EXPERT AUTHORITY

THE NEW, ADVANCED (& EASIER) WAY TO PUBLISH A BOOK AND GET AS MANY CUSTOMERS, CLIENTS AND SALES AS YOU CAN HANDLE...

Even if you hate writing, even if you hate selling, struggled in the past and even if you don't think you're an expert...

JOHN MULRY, MSC

JOHN MULRY, MSC

What others are saying...

"John was lucky enough to be personally mentored and trained by me. As a GKIC Certified Business Advisor, he's equipped with an arsenal of tools that any small business owner can pick up and run with to start producing big time, bottom line results. This is exactly the kind of advice I needed when I started my career... but nobody who really knew what was going on was willing to share. If you're a business owner and you want real improvement in your business then I highly suggest you listen to what John has to say."
  – **Dan Kennedy, Dan Kennedy, Serial Entrepreneur, Multi Millionaire and Highest Paid Direct Response Marketer in the World**

"The thing about John that most people aren't willing to do, is to actually apply the best practices that they learn to their own business and life in order to achieve maximum effectiveness in minimum time." **- Nick Nanton, CEO of the Dicks Nanton Celebrity Branding® Agency, Emmy Award Winning Director, Producer & Best-Selling Author**

"I've worked with John before and when he told me he was releasing Expert Authority I was on board straight away. I've been through similar programs before but most of them were very vague and they had a lot of hype at the start but not too much information and definitely none of the follow up. Expert Authority walks you through every step of the way. A child could do it. It'll definitely help you get more clients." **– Keith Caverley**

"Right from the very first interaction I had with John, which was getting his book "Truth About Marketing" all the way to someone to one consultation time, I have been blown away by the actionable advice I have received. Even if I implement just a few things he suggested, it will add €1,000's to my income over the coming months and years. He's one of the most knowledgeable and sincere marketers around." **- Gareth Sherry**

It didn't take long for John's marketing gems to click on a few light bulbs for me and set me straight, as I put together my new advertising campaigns. Yep, light bulbs is a good metaphor - I feel as if a whole series of darkened mind corridors have been illuminated and revealed! But that's not all. John was so generous in contacting me personally to sort out some tech issues, a great reflection of his generosity in sharing his expertise and giving value to so many."
- **Audrey Wynne**

"Working with John, he helped me develop some simple but very effective sales and marketing strategies that have helped me close sales and increase revenue for my business. John's in depth knowledge of marketing and his easy to apply systems are a huge benefit to any business needing a boost. Highly recommended."
- **Don Neachtain**

"Surpassed my expectations so much that I am in awe (I have never used that word in m life). One of the most helpful contacts I have ever had with any marketing consultant and I have years of personal experience with consultants - a few in the excellent category, so I am not just comparing him to the usual ones but to the best."
- **Lee Parratt**

"John provides quality information for anyone who is in business, or looking to get into business, concerning their marketing efforts. I follow everything John Mulry and Dan Kennedy teach in their marketing training. It is amazing what little changes they teach can do for a business." – **Brian Whitesides**

For more visit www.JohnMulry.com

EXPERT AUTHORITY

JOHN MULRY, MSC

ISBN-13: 978-0-9928003-6-9

Expert AUTHORity is available at special quantity discounts for bulk purchases, for sales promotions, premiums, fundraising, and educational use. For more information, please write to the below address.

Published by: Expect Success Academy, Unit 14, Ballybane Enterprise Centre, Ballybane, Galway, Ireland

www.expertauthorityformula.com

First Edition, 2017

Edited by: Jessica Thompson - www.Jessica.ie

Cover Art by: Sam and Bax

Published in Ireland

Make sure you attend the advanced (and easier) 'THUD FACTOR' Method training online at…

www.expertauthorityformula.com/register

In life, you don't necessarily get what you want and you don't necessarily get what you need. Instead, you get what you honestly and truly believe you deserve. In other words, you get what you expect, so why not EXPECT SUCCESS?

–John Mulry

Table of Contents

EXPERT AUTHORITY

Preface

"I'm going to write a book"

"I know. You said you always would".

"No I'm going to write it and finish it by the end of the month".

"What?" "That won't be easy".

"I know, but I'm going to do it anyway".

And I did. It didn't take a month though. All in all it took me 20 days to finish my first book *Your Elephant's Under Threat*, and writing turned out to be one of the best things I've ever done for myself and my business.

That was back in early September 2013.

I arrived home to my girlfriend Jess on a rare sunny evening from the office and before I even said hi, I uttered those words.

I had uttered them before, but this time was different. This time I meant business. This time I wasn't just going to think about writing a book, I was going to ACTUALLY do it.

And I planned on doing it by the end of September.

And on the 22nd of September my manuscript was finished. In no way was it the next installment of Harry Potter but as you'll discover, it didn't and doesn't need to be.

It needed some edits, a glamorous cover and some marketing magic, but it was DONE. From idea to implementation in just shy of 21 days.

I've since finished FIVE more books (including this one) and contributed to multiple others with no plans of stopping any time soon.

I share this story because if you're reading this I can safely assume that at some point you too have thought of writing THAT book.

I do believe everyone has at least one book in them.

And in this book, it's my goal to provide you the framework to take your idea for THAT book and turn it into more than idea.

Turn it into something that makes your potential clients go "WOW" when it lands on their table, office desk or lap.

Yes, inside these pages I'm going to unearth for you, the secrets to writing a book that probably won't win you any writing awards but I promise if you follow the advice, guidance, strategies and resources inside this book, you'll have your very own blueprint for writing a book that has your IDEAL clients chomping at the bit to do business with you.

And I'm going to share with you, why writing a book needn't be as daunting or as drawn out as you might think, in fact I'm going to share with you how you can start and finish a book in as little as 7 days.

I'll share with you the why, the multiple how's, the what's and I'll even outline strategies to use for when your book is finished because as you're about to discover – writing a book is just the first step of some exciting client getting steps that come afterwards.

You invested in this book which was step one, now you're on step 2 – consumption, the final and most important is action.

Enjoy, take lots of notes then most importantly take lots of ACTION.

And if you feel like fast tracking your results and/or getting my advanced training, or applying for my expert authority coaching / done for you programs full details are available towards the end of this book.

Thanks for reading – John Mulry

EXPERT AUTHORITY

Part I - WHY You Should Write a Business Book...

When you're running a business, either as a one man army or as part of a team – your time is finite so I understand if you think you've other priorities on your plate ahead of writing THAT book you've always wanted to write.

The thing is though, writing a book is an investment. It's an investment in yourself and in your business.

As you're about to discover, writing a business book with the goal for client generation really is one of those rare activities where you do the work once and you can profit from it again and again.

Much like building marketing systems, marketing and sales assets in your business there are few activities that you can TRULY profit again and again after the fact.

The majority of your day is no doubt taken up with putting out fires, dealing with staff who don't do what they're getting paid to do, vendors and suppliers who don't do what they say they'll do.

For instance, I've had one client get stuck with a marketing company who promised the world, charge him thousands upon thousands and didn't deliver anything in a TWO YEAR period. He then sought me out and in 5 days I accomplished more than the other company (pack of charlatans) did in two years.

So I get it if you've a LOT on but I'm going to convince you that if you're in business and you're in a competitive niche and you wish you had more clients coming through your door then there's no better tool to use in marketing your business than your very own book.

In fact, I'm going to outline SEVEN different reasons why you should write a business book, each on their own carries a compelling enough argument but compounded will paint a very clear picture as to how important a book can be for your business.

If after you read these SEVEN different reasons you aren't convinced, I'd suggest you close this book and pass it along to someone who will use it.

That may be harsh but like I mentioned, your time is finite, no point spending it (wisely) reading this if you haven't bought into the notion whatsoever.

7 Reasons You Should Write a Business Book

1. It's the ULTIMATE Lead Generation Tool

Two types of marketing…

For me there are two types of marketing: EFFECTIVE and INEFFECTIVE.

That's it. Your marketing either works or it doesn't.

Anybody that says otherwise is probably selling you snake oil or trying to sell you into the notion that you need to keep advertising (the same boring ineffective crap) to build up awareness of your brand and blah blah blah!

Brand marketing works BUT only if you've the budget needed to keep up the repetition. I cover why this is and what to do about it (so you're advertising and marketing is PROFITABLE) in my second book *The Truth!*

The bottom line is this:

When you're running a small business, you can't afford to spend money on marketing and advertising and HOPE your phone rings or HOPE you make a sale – you need to know whether or not your marketing gets results. Period.

This is where Direct Response marketing comes in.

Direct Response marketing is marketing that elicits a DIRECT response be it a lead or a sale.

And the backbone of direct response marketing is lead generation.

And a book that positions you as the AUTHORITY is the ULTIMATE lead generation tool.

Lead generation marketing is essentially marketing and advertising in such a way that has your most IDEAL clients put their hands up and say *"Yes! I'm interested in what you have to offer, please tell me more"*.

It can be done online and offline (and best done in a combination of both). It's truly one of the best ways to market your business for three reasons.

1. You can access lists and markets easily no matter what your product or service.
2. You build a database of INTERESTED prospects which you can follow up with.
3. It can provide insane ROI when done correctly.

The best form of lead generation is advertising something of VALUE to your target audience. For example a book that solves a problem or helps them make a better decision as it relates to doing business with you is one of the best forms of lead generation.

You attract a certain type of client with a lead generating book...

Another reason why a book makes the Ultimate Lead Generation tool is that it attracts a certain type of buyer.

Book buyers and book readers make for excellent clients.

Why?

They're curious, they invest in themselves and they're constantly looking for information, looking for ways to improve themselves be it their bodies, their lives, their relationships, their health, their business, their well being.

Those who invest in themselves and read books, go to events, do courses will prove to be your best clients.

And people who invest in themselves gravitate towards experts, gravitate toward leaders and aren't afraid to pay for things either.

People who don't invest in themselves, who want everything handed to them make for lousy clients, they'll shop based on price and will try and haggle you down to the bone to save a few dimes.

I don't do business with those types and neither should you.

They're more invested in you – much better than a tweet

The more time a potential client invests in you, in your marketing and sales process the better because they're hard wired into you, into your way of doing things.

If someone takes the time to read your book and you've put the right elements into it (which we'll discuss further on) the more inclined they'll be to want to do business with you.

For example, read this snippet of a testimonial I received for my second book The Truth!

> *"This book has literally transformed the way I think about marketing and the way I approach it. **John's book is so digestible, so easy to read, it's nearly like you know the man. The way he communicates the information in the book is so easy to follow.** He really puts you in the mindset of the buyer or prospect. John brings it back to simple techniques of what people want and what they need.*

Pay attention to the line: *"it's nearly like you know the man"*.

At the time, I hadn't met the person who left that feedback (I since have) but he felt like he knew me, just from reading the words I put down on paper.

That's powerful stuff and with your book you'll do the same.

2. *Unlock The Power of The A.C.E. Formula*

Having your own business book is the Ultimate Form of positioning in your business. You can utilize the magic of the A.C.E. Formula which is the second reason you should write a book for your business.

What is the A.C.E. formula?

Well it stands for:

- Authority
- Celebrity
- Expert

If you are not actively and consistently positioning yourself as the AUTHORITY, the CELEBRITY and the EXPERT in your marketplace then you are seriously missing out.

Frank Kern one of the most talented and charismatic marketers of our time has this to say about AUTHORITY:

"Authority – possibly one of the most influential market positions one could ever hold. Think about it, a person of authority tells us to go do something; we often unquestioningly go do it because they told us to." - Frank Kern

One of the BIGGEST reasons why many businesses fail is because they have no… **AUTHORITY.**

It doesn't matter if you have the best idea ever, if no one buys it, you're not going to make any money…

Having authority in a market, means people will listen to you…

It's the same with **CELEBRITY.**

You can and should be using the art of celebrity in your business as much as possible.

Think about it, the highest paid people on earth are celebrities right? They get paid seemingly obscene amounts of money just because of who they are and what they can do.

Now I'm not claiming you can go out there and be the next Kim Kardashian or 'The Rock' Dwayne Johnson but there's absolutely nothing stopping you from positioning yourself and strategically using celebrity in your business so your target customers see you as a celebrity.

To do so you need to have the third component of the A.C.E. formula in play: **EXPERT.**

There's an old saying: *"It's not WHAT you know, it's WHO you know."* Like most old sayings, there's an element of truth to it. But what's missing is the related truth: The more WHOs that know WHAT you know, the more money you'll make.

In other words the more people who view and see you as an expert the more leads you'll generate, the more sales you'll make, the more clients you'll convert and the more money you'll make.

The trick is to get comfortable with who you are… and who you are not.

1. What do you do better than anybody?
2. What do you do well?
3. What do you do adequately?
4. What do you do so badly, it's embarrassing?

Take the time to actually answer those four questions then put all your focus in 1 and 2 and then outsource the rest or partner with or pay other who can do them for you.

So how do you become an expert?

Well you can become an expert through the following:

- Legitimate personal experience
- Read the top ten books in the field
- Read two years of industry journal back issues
- Join trade associations
- Attend a major trade show, convention, or conference
- Attend an industry leader's seminar
- Keep a notebook of unanswered questions - then get them answered
- Seek out several leaders in the industry and consult with them personally (informally or formally)

Becoming an expert is ONLY HALF THE BATTLE.

Arguably the more important half is being RECOGNISED as an expert. You can be recognized as an expert by the following:

- **WRITE A BOOK**
- Create information products.
- Do high profile advertising in industry journals.
- Launch a publicity campaign.
- Write articles for industry journals.
- Speak at industry conferences and/or market and conduct your own seminars.
- Publish a newsletter.
- Surround yourself with recognized experts by having them write for your newsletter, speak at your seminars, interview them for audio products, podcasts etc.

AUTHORITY, CELEBRITY and EXPERT combined equal the A.C.E. formula and there is no better strategy for attracting and converting your most ideal clients.

Out of all of the ways to become recognized as an expert there is no better than having your own book. Not only does it make you the **EXPERT but it ALSO gives you MASSIVE AUTHORITY and CELEBRITY.**

WRITING A BOOK can be the fastest most powerful and profitable way to gain authority, celebrity and expertise in your niche.

3. Having a book allows you to share your story and your philosophy

Ideas can be copied, business models can be copied, products and services can be copied but the one thing that you have that CANNOT be copied is you.

You would do well to remember that.

Best of all by actually sharing what's unique about you, sharing your unique story and journey you can connect with your clients on a whole other level - even if what you offer is seemingly mundane and or boring.

You can turn the boring into exciting by sharing your story and a book allows you and gives you the platform to do that.

By right, your philosophy and story shouldn't matter. If you have a product or service that can help people that should be enough right? But to the consumer your philosophy and story do matter.

Your potential clients hunger for philosophical compatibility and you can give it to them in spades in your book.

These days now more than ever the number one currency is TRUST.

Your potential clients want to trust someone they think they understand, (mostly) agree with, respect, admire and are interested in.

If you're still relying on *just* facts, figures, features and benefits you will soon find those wells drying up as competition gets tougher and tougher.

By understanding what your philosophy is and then sharing it (along with your story) in a book you'll bond with your potential clients on a whole other level.

Here's an example:

One of my most popular articles ever is my 67 things you didn't know about John Mulry articles.

It was essentially an article where I dove deep into me, my world, my ups, downs and everything in between.

And mentioned very little to do with business.

I published this and the feedback was incredible.

I attracted people, I repelled people (not a bad thing), I insulted people, I offended people, I embarrassed myself, I share some very personal moments all in a way that's unique to me.

If you were to read it, you too may be attracted, offended or even disgusted – the thing is all of that is ok.

I have a certain philosophy I live by and it's something I try and live every day.

Naturally I have shitty days too where I feel the walls are caving in and I feel like I'm getting nowhere but more often than not I start each day EXPECTING SUCCESS.

My philosophy is this:

In life, you don't necessarily get what you want and you don't necessarily get what you need. Instead, you get what you honestly and truly believe you deserve. In other words, you get what you expect, so why not EXPECT SUCCESS?

What is your philosophy? How can you utilize your past and present life experiences and personal story to connect with prospects, customers and clients?

In my first book *Your Elephant's Under Threat* I shared how I came to discover that philosophy through a life of bullying, low self esteem, failure after failure until I finally started doing things for myself.

As well as sharing some interesting highlights and stories along the way from volunteering for a year in South America, ending up in jail in Brazil, discovering fitness, writing, marketing and more.

If you're interested in reading it, you can get a free copy of at www.JohnMulry.com – you just pay the low shipping and handling fee.

One thing I want to mention is when you start to share your philosophy be it in your own book, online or in person – you will alienate people, you will repel people and there will be those people who won't like it.

My advice: forget about them.

If your philosophy is true to you, then truly forget about those who aren't attracted to it.

Why?

Because those who are, those who do like your philosophy will also like you.

And if they like you – there's a VERY strong probability they'll want to do business with you.

A book that shares your honesty, your ups and downs, your humanity, and your interests is a fantastic lead generating tool to have in your arsenal.

Here are six concrete reasons why sharing your story and philosophy in a book will lead you to getting more clients:

1. People distrust, don't like and are uncomfortable with lawyers, salespeople, doctors, etc., and maybe you too. A book helps establish that trust.
2. A book humanizes you. It makes you approachable, someone to confide in, and someone with compassion.
3. It suggests having a broader conversation with you than business matters.
4. It makes you an interesting person.
5. It suggests maturity and stability.
6. It elevates you above your competition.

Remember, people trust for irrational reasons.

WHO you ARE is far more important than what you do.

People want to "feel good about" the person they get advice from, buy products from, or in some way let into their life.

On a purely rational, logical basis no client should care about any of this.

But we're more irrational, more emotional than rational and logical when it comes to trust and when it comes to making decisions.

Every business can benefit from telling their story and there's no better format than in your own book.

4. A book raises you (and your prices) ABOVE your competitors.

Having your own book that tells your story, shares your philosophy, helps your prospects get informed and make better decisions elevates you above your competition in a way they won't see coming.

Your competitors are all out there advertising their businesses badly, all competing against each other over the few available 'now buyers' in your marketplace whereas you, when you have a business book and follow my model will stand above them by ACTUALLY advertising something of value to your target audience (your book). This will attract the best types of prospects to you.

Prospects that will both convert immediately and those who won't ensuring you have a pipeline of leads of varying gestation so you'll always have a constant stream of potential clients to do business with.

The how of all of this (in case you're wondering) is covered in later chapters.

5. You can build a list of BUYERS with your book.

Here's something I've learned from my mentor Dan Kennedy which I've cemented into my little Irish brain:

A buyer is a buyer is a buyer is a buyer…

What Dan means is; when someone buys from you, they will continue to buy from you as long as you're not afraid to make offers and those offers make their lives, easier, better, faster and it adds value to them.

Obviously not everyone will buy everything but a buyer lead is highly more valuable than a normal lead.

Both have value but the buyer lead more so.

Using you book at the beginning of your sales process, say in a free plus shipping offer (where you send the book for free but the buyer pays shipping) they're self qualifying themselves as someone who is interested in what you have to offer and is willing to spend money on that interest.

With a strategic ladder of ascension in your business you can ascend those initial buyers up your ladder and exchange more value for more profits.

For example – one of my funnels starts with a free + shipping book offer, then some training then the offer of a paid consultation then private coaching and/or done for you marketing implementation.

The book is the perfect entry point and it can be for you too no matter what ladder of ascension model you follow.

Here are some ideas and example value ladders and ascension models you could follow:

1. Free plus shipping book offer > invite to webinar / live event > high end offer / coaching
2. Front end book offer > free / paid consultation / high end programs
3. Free plus shipping book offer > more in depth training, continuity program > high end service / coaching / offer

These are just some samples but the key is that your building a list of BUYERS with your book and with consistently adding value and making offers you can ascend them up your ladder of ascension and increase the value they get and the profits you generate.

6. When you have your own book you become an information marketer

When you transition from merely advertising your business into someone who advertises something of value to your target audience (namely useful information in the form of your book) you transform yourself from a normal business into an information marketing business.

Using information marketing in your business is one of the best strategies you can use (no matter what your business or industry).

Why? Well for starters here are three reasons:

1. Materials perceived as information are better received and given more attention than materials perceived as just advertising.
2. Salespeople have sales literature. Trusted advisors have information.
3. Advertising free or nearly free, useful information is a low-threshold offer.

Typical advertising and marketing that doesn't offer anything of value but merely advertises the business is only attracting a very small percentage of people in your target audience.

High threshold offers like a visit with a salesman, a test drive or dental exam are useful but solely using them means you're missing out on and deterring a large proportion of people who would otherwise be interested in what you have to offer.

Again refer to my book *The Truth!* to dive into this.

7. A Book is Easy to Say Yes To

No matter if you're the greatest salesman in the world, selling high ticket items (say product services larger than $1K+) is very difficult right off the bat.

Sure it can be done, yes, of course it can.

But when you're the guy or gal who literally wrote the book on (insert your product or service) it's infinitely easier.

Remember the point I made about sharing your story and your philosophy and the fact that people naturally gravitate and seek out experts? When you have your own book you're accomplishing all of that.

So let me ask you – who's going to have a better chance of closing clients on high ticket offers – they guy who goes straight to pitch, pitch, pitch or the guy (or gal) who's put in the leg work ahead of time, positions himself as the authority, celebrity and expert and who literally wrote the book on the topic.

Easy answer right?

I hope you're starting to realise how powerful a book can be for your business and if these reasons aren't enough – like I said maybe this book isn't for you. Feel free to pass it on. No hard feelings.

Now you know WHY a book is _that_ important for your business, it's time dive deep into HOW to actually go about writing a book.

There are a number of methods I'm going to walk you through.

Don't feel like you have to stick to just one.

For example, a large proportion of this book was written on a flight I took to Phoenix from Ireland.

A client flew me over to work on some campaigns, funnels and systems in his business for the week and I utilized the first method I'm going to share with you to get this book done.

Part II – The HOW of Writing Your Business Book

When it comes to sitting down to actually write your book that's where a lot of people fall down. However the writing of your book is much easier than you think. There are many different methods you can use to write your book but I'm going to walk you through some of the quickest and the easiest. Some of these methods will be new to you and others you may have come across before – all methods will be valid though.

There's lots of books and information out there on and writing books and publishing books but not all of them actually go into a lot of detail on *actually* how to write the book. What wI want to do in this section is break down the 'how to' of writing and make it as easy as possible for you.

Remember the aim of the book you are writing is not to be the next *Harry Potter* or the next *Lord of the Rings.* You're writing a book that's going to position you as the ultimate authority, expert and celebrity in your industry.

Obviously the book does have to add value to your target audience and the content and expertise you share in the book will do that (especially when you follow my section on what to write about) but it doesn't have to be this massive undertaking that takes forever or that completely consumes your time.

When you use the methods I'm going to share with you, over the next few pages you WILL get your book finished very quickly. What I want stress beforehand though is to make sure you pick whichever method is best suited to you and your situation. By all means experiment with the different methods but if this is your first time writing a book – choose a method you're most comfortable with.

Titles, Subtitles and More

Every one of my books start out the same way – I write out the title (or working title) and the subtitle either on a sheet of blank paper or I type them into a blank word document. The reason I do this is so I can visually see my book whether it's on my computer, desktop or a sheet of paper.

Having the title in your head is one thing but when you write it out and commit it to paper it starts to become more real and it starts the creative juices flowing. Plus you'll see how the title reads and you can read it aloud to hear how it sounds. These things while they may sound minor are very important.

Plus when you get the title and subtitle down on paper you'll be starting the brainstorming process. You'll probably never settle on your first title but that's ok.

If you're having a hard time coming up with titles here are four quick and easy tips you can use:

1. Look at some of the top selling titles in your industry – model them.

2. Use 'How to' titles that solve your target audiences biggest problem(s)
3. Use benefit driven titles or titles that help your target audience avoid pain.
4. Use the element of curiosity in your title but then explain things in your subtitle.

For example, my first book the title is *"Your Elephant's Under Threat"*, it's certainly not clear what the book is about but the subtitle makes it very easy to understand what the core of the book is about.

Once you have your Title and Subtitle the next thing you're going to want to do is what I call "Book Blueprinting"

Book Blueprinting:

Blueprinting is simply taking your title and subtitle and expanding on them. You're going to take the core topic of your book and split it into elements. The number of elements is really up to you but for simplistic purposes you can use say 5, 7, 11, 13 elements.

Now, in reality you can use more if you like, it's completely up to you. Don't get too hung up on the how many, just split your core topic into as many logical sub topics as necessary. These sub topics now become the basis for the chapters in your book.

Say for example, if I was writing a book on Facebook Advertising – some of the sub elements of this book may be the following:

1. Why Facebook
2. Facebook Advertising Overview
3. Creating The Perfect Campaign
4. Choosing Your Target Audience
5. Creating The Perfect Ad
6. Facebook Retargeting

7. Case Studies and FAQ

You see I've taken the core topic of Facebook Advertising and split it into seven sub topics or sub elements. Pretty easy so far right?

Once you have the sub elements of your book mapped out into chapter topics the next step is simply split your chapter topics into bullet points. You can have as many or as few bullet points as you need here. Again don't get too hung up on the number just make sure you get your message across.

Once you have bullet pointed each of your chapters you have the blueprint of your book pretty much finalized and believe it or not – the hard work is done.

Blueprinting allows you to quickly and easily map out your book into small manageable chunks while and lets you pretty much see and play with the flow of your book before you sit down to write any of the content. The art of blueprinting makes the actually writing of your book a whole lot easier and the process can be done in about 10 - 20 mins.

Once you have your book blueprinted the next step for you to take is to write a simple promotional description for the book. Again don't get too hung up on the length here but remember it's just a description of your book not a chapter in itself. Focus on the describing the topic of your book, the direct benefits of reading it as well as being clear who it's for (and who it's not for) and then include a call to action.

After you have completed the title, subtitle, the book blueprint and promotional description – all you have to focus on is fleshing out each of the bullet points in your chapters and add the essentials (which I'll be discussing a little later) and hey presto – your book is done.

Now I know what you're thinking – this part is easy but how do I go about writing the rest of the book and how do I go about fleshing out the rest of it once I have completed the other steps.

That's what we're going to discuss now.

How to write your book, fast!

In this section I'm going to share with you four different but equally powerful methods for writing your book fast.

Each method has its advantages and disadvantages but like I mentioned choose which ever method you find your most comfortable and don't get too hung up on any if you think you wouldn't be able for it.

The first method is what I call:

The Blunt Force Method

This method is the one I used to write my very first book *Your Elephant's Under Threat*. The method is as it sounds – a blunt force method for writing as it involves some serious time blocking where you give nearly 100% focus to the writing of your book until it's done.

Whether that time is one day, two days, 7 days or like in my case 21 days – that doesn't matter.

What matters is you put the goal of writing your book as your #1 focus and you keep it like that until it's done.

Now a fair warning – this method isn't for everyone as it obviously requires dedication and focus.

But the good thing is once you decide to use this method you kind of go into a possessed frenzy of writing.

I remember coming home to Jess and telling her I was going to write a book by the end of the month and all I could think about was writing my book.

Obviously I still took care other tasks but my main priority was the book and the sense of urgency and enthusiasm made the whole writing process that much easier.

I guess it's like when you're going on holiday.

Before you leave there's always a 101 things that need to be done but you always, always get everything done just in time and you go on holidays without a hitch. **It's the power of having a big deadline.**

The blunt force method of writing uses the same psychological triggers and it can help you get your book done very quickly. After all if your book is only 50 – 100 pages – there's nothing stopping you using the blunt force method and writing your book over the course of 1 or 2 all nighters. Not exactly easy but very achievable.

Obviously when you finish the book it will still need editing (which you won't be doing) and will still need a cover as well as the essentials but the hard work will be done.

The Overnight Method:

The second method I'm going to walk you through is an ingenious method for a number of reasons:

1. You can literally have your book done overnight
2. You can get feedback on your book and tweak to suit your audience before it's even published
3. You can get supplementary content and creative's for your book created alongside your book
4. It doesn't involve any "writing" per se.

Sounds great right? It's actually the method I used to write my second book The Truth!

That book hit the top sellers in the marketplace where I launched it for three days in a row.

What's the method? Well it simply involves taking your book blueprint and turning it into a webinar.

Here are the steps:

1. You take your book blueprint and turn it into a webinar presentation.
2. You create a PowerPoint presentation using your blueprint as the skeleton.
3. You choose a date a time for your webinar.
4. You promote your webinar and get registrations (either to your list if you have one or by advertising if you don't)
5. You present your webinar (talking through each point) and record it.
6. Afterwards you get the webinar recording transcribed and edited (by someone else – not you).
7. Voila! You now have the guts of your book done. Add the essentials and a cover and you're done.
8. BONUS 1: Ask webinar attendees for feedback, testimonials to use in the promotion of your book.
9. BONUS 2: Use the audio or video of your webinar as bonus content for buyers of your book.

See, I told you it was a pretty ingenious method of creating your book. Notice I said creating and not writing because with this method you're not really sitting down to do any strict writing.

If you're used to doing webinars or presentations this method will work really well for you.

I'd also like to point out that there are quite a number of books (some New York Times Bestsellers too by the way) that have used this exact method and you probably would never have known otherwise.

The Everyday Method

This method is fairly self explanatory and straightforward. It involves simply writing every day. Be it an hour (or more) every morning or every night it doesn't matter you simply get into the habit of writing every day and before you know it you'll be knocking out chapters and books in no time at all.

Stephen King has documented in his must read book (*Stephen King On Writing*) that he writes for 4 hours a day 365 days a year. Any wonder he has so many books written?

Now you don't have to write for 4 hours but maybe start with an hour or say 1,000 words. You'd be surprised how many words you can actually write in an hour (with a bit of practice).

And you can write a hell of a lot more when you're working off your book blueprint which you've already created.

Using the everyday method probably won't be your first choice but it is the one I recommend.

Writing is like any skill and the more you practice it the stronger, the faster and the better you'll get at it. It's like working a muscle, the more you work it, the stronger and healthier it gets.

Personally I like to write every day for an hour (usually in the morning). Now I don't keep to this religiously and I might go days without writing but I don't get too hung up on things if I miss some days.

The key isn't perfection. The key is getting things done. I use a combination of methods and I use many tools from my arsenal to get the job or project done.

What I also like to do alongside this method is keep an idea journal or notepad. I actually use a real notepad and my smart phone for this so I can take notes on any ideas for content or projects I might get.

Better to get your ideas down on paper. Whether or not you get to implement them is another thing but one thing is for sure, if you can't remember the idea, there's no chance in hell you'll implement it right?

The simple act of writing your ideas down will make you more creative while also allowing your brain a bit of room and breathing space. That's why brain dumping works so well. It's like giving your creative juices a clean slate.

You never know when you might get that million dollar idea, it could while in the gym, while walking your dog or while sipping coffee. Writing it down there and then could make the difference between idea implementation and idea death.

In fact, the idea for another book I hope to release soon came at the most random of times.

I was on holidays with Jess visiting one of our most favourite places to go. It's a place called the Aran Islands on the west coast of Ireland.

Three little islands of untouched, raw Irish beauty.

You have to get a ferry from across which takes about 40 minutes.

When we were crossing the weather was a little choppy so Jess decided to go to the upper deck to get some fresh air.

There was also a couple of Americans sitting in front of us who thought it would be a good idea to bring Nutella sandwiches onto the ferry. The stench of their sandwiches was filling the ferry and was making Jess a little queasy.

As she was on the upper deck trying not to get sick I was down below giving the American my best look of disdain when I started thinking about the conversation I had with a friend a few days earlier.

We were talking about possible projects and he asked me how I keep so productive and the fact he and a lot of his clients really struggle to get and stay organized.

Then it hit me. I should write a book about that.

I started blueprinting the book there and then and before Jess came back down I had the blueprint for the book there and then. I simply used the built in notes app on my phone to blueprint everything and later emailed it to myself.

Done and it took less than 10 minutes.

That's the power of always being ready to take note of your ideas and start the process of implementation.

Taking notes on your ideas isn't just something you can use with The Everyday Method – it's something I recommend you do regardless.

The Speak Your Book Method

The fourth method of writing is the Speak Your Book Method.

This method while fairly self explanatory is quite similar to the overnight method.

Instead of creating a full on webinar on your topic you would simply take your book blueprint and record yourself speaking through each of your chapter bullet points.

You could either do this all in one go or schedule out an hour or so for each chapter. Then at the scheduled time take out your smart phone, a Dictaphone or your computer and record yourself talking through each element.

Once you recorded all your sessions you send them off to be transcribed and edited and hey presto you're done.

You simply add in the essentials, get a cover created and your book is finished.

Once again, this method is very simple and it involves little to no actual writing. You may think of this method or the overnight method as 'cheating'.

If you do, all I say is – get over it.

The content you are CREATING is all your own, it's your expertise – you're just using technology and hired help to turn that content into the written word.

You shouldn't have any hang up over it and it allows you to complete your book arguably faster than you ever would otherwise.

Summary

At the end of the day, choose whichever one you find yourself gravitating towards and have some fun with it.

As long as what you creates solves your target markets problem, helps them, adds value to them and positions you as the expert and authority you are – who cares what method you use right?

I would like to stress this important point however!

Whichever method you do choose – make sure you complete the initial steps of blueprinting your book or else everything will be an unorganized mess.

Note: To get a full walkthrough of each of the above methods (along with actionable templates and worksheets and done for you resources) make sure you first register for the THUD FACTOR training and then if you're ready enroll in the full Expert Authority Formula program. To register for the THUD FACTOR webinar visit www.expertauthorityformula.com/register

The Nine Essentials to EVERY Book:

One point I've mentioned a few times over the last few pages are "The Essentials".

Now, you may be wondering – what the hell are the essentials? If you have been, don't worry Watson I'm going to walk you through each and every one of them now. The essentials are the ESSENTIAL supplementary elements that you NEED to include in your book.

First and foremost they actually make your book a fully-fledged book but they clearly position you as the authority, celebrity and expert while also make it easy for your readers (prospects) to take the next step in your sales process be that request a consultation, visit your website, call your office, join your membership or whatever.

The Nine Essentials are the following:
1. Table of Contents
2. Copyright Page
3. About The Author
4. Who You Help
5. Introduction
6. Testimonials

7. Next Steps
8. Also From The Author
9. Back Cover Copy and Description

Let's go through each one:

1. Table of Contents

This one is pretty self explanatory and in fact – it's easy because you can take this directly from your book blueprint. Straightforward but no doubt essential right?

2. Copyright Page

This is a straight forward page that states all of the pertinent information of your book along with your contact details and things like ISBN number etc. If you want to see an example simply look at the one at the beginning of this book.

3. About The Author

Your book will also need an About the Author section which is essentially you and your business' bio. Here's a surefire winning tip. Instead of writing your bio in the traditional boring method of simply talking about yourself, do the following:

- Write your bio in such a way that describes what you do to HELP your target audience instead of simply stating what it is you do.
- Call out specifically who you help, how you help them and state some social proof elements that can back up what you claim. For example board certified, featured in a magazine, radio or TV shows etc.
- Inject some of your personality and something a little lighter into your bio. For example mention your family or where you live etc.
- Include a call to action (the next step you want them to take). For example to request a free consultation visit www.yourwebsite.com

4. Who You Help

It's important to have a section in your book (either an extended bio or standalone section) that details exactly WHO you help and HOW you help them.

This is where you get to inject your uniqueness and what makes you different in the marketplace. Don't be vague.

For example don't say *"I'm a financial planner and I help people with their pensions"*.

Instead say something like:

I help professional men and women aged 55 and up ensure they avoid the financial pitfalls which come with retirement. My proprietary 11 point profitable pension plan gives them complete peace of mind knowing their family and financial needs will be taken care of before and after their retirement.

See the difference? I know who I'd prefer to talk to.

5. Book Introduction

Your book introduction will serve as a simple but enticing hook to get them excited to turn the page. Keep it simple, tell them what they're going discover by reading your book and give them overview of what you'll be covering. Also don't be afraid to direct them to your website if they want further help (or whatever your call to action may be).

6. Testimonials

Testimonials and social proof are massive and when used right can make the difference between someone doing business with you and someone not. Including testimonials in your book are another great way to hammer home your authority and expertise.

You have three options here.

- Include endorsements and testimonials on the book itself
- Include testimonials on you and your business
- A combination of both

> To get my perfect testimonial blueprint – which details the exact questions that ensure you get the best testimonial ever every time, send a picture of yourself and your copy of Expert Authority to John@JohnMulry.com or tag me in a post on Facebook.

7. Next Steps

At the end of your book and possibly in the last chapter of your book you want to include a "Your Next Steps" section. This would simply summarize what your reader has learned while also outlining some recommended next steps they should take.

Obviously one of the steps should be to contact you (or whatever the next step in your sales process is) if they want to fast track their results.

8. Also From The Author

This section simply gives an overview of your other products and/or services you have on offer.

9. Back Cover Copy

The Back Cover Copy is the copy that goes on the back of your book cover. This needs to really hook your potential readers in and clearly give the main benefits your book provides. The Back Cover copy will also help you in creating your sales and promotional materials to go along with your book.

That covers the 'How to' of writing your book. Hopefully you're starting to get excited and you've already begun to get a flood of ideas for your own book of books.

In the next section we're going to focus on WHAT to write about. And we're going to do so in a way that really allows your expertise to shine through.

EXPERT AUTHORITY

Part III: What to Write About

Like I've mentioned a few times there are a lot of books out there on writing books but very few offer any practical, usable information. Similarly there are a lot of books that help you on the mechanics of writing a book but fail to help you on the content side of things i.e. WHAT to actually write about.

In this section I'm going to go over some very simple but very powerful strategies you can use for the content of your book. Again, I recommend you use whichever method you're most comfortable with or if you can even combine some elements.

Remember, these methods are just strategies – you're the expert and you already have the expertise and content inside of you – these methods just make it easy for you to take that expertise and turn it into a book.

Here are five methods you can use for the content of your book. Now these aren't the only methods you can use but they are quick and easy methods.

The Afraid To Ask Method:

The first method is so easy you'll kick yourself for not thinking of it sooner. In fact, all five methods are really easy but this one can be done in no time at all.

I first learned a variation of this method from Mike Koenigs years ago – he used it for video but I adapted it to be used in written form and it works equally as well today as it did when I first heard it.

You have FAQ's and SAQ's. FAQ's stands for Frequently Asked Questions and SAQs stands for Should Ask Questions.

The afraid the ask method combines all of the questions you get from potential and existing clients/customers with all of the questions you WISH your potential clients/customers would ask.

You write down all of your FAQs and all of your SAQs and yes you guessed it you simply answer them.

All of them. You'll more than likely come up with anywhere from 20 – 100 questions which you answer.

What you're doing is creating a master document (book) that works at educating and pre selling your target customers ahead of time while also allowing you to actively overcome all typical objections your potential clients/customers have to doing business with you.

It's pure genius.

The questions and answers become the core of your book. You add the essentials, get a cover created and you're done.

You can then call this book:

"Everything you ever wanted to know about X (your topic) but were afraid to ask."

Best of all you don't have to learn anything new – you're simply answering questions on your own expertise and turning it into a book.

You can use this method for literally every industry or business and it's so easy.

Here are some more examples:

- "Everything you ever want to know about starting an online business but were afraid to ask."
- "Everything you ever want to know about taxation for your business but were afraid to ask."
- "Everything you ever want to know about online marketing but were afraid to ask."
- "Everything you ever want to know about network marketing but were afraid to ask."
- "Everything ever want to know about X but were afraid to ask"

The Afraid To Ask method is a very easy way of extracting the expertise inside of your brain and it doesn't take a lot of work.

If you're struggling when it comes to writing a book this is definitely one method I'd highly recommend you use.

The Interview Method:

The second method is the interview method. This method lets you utilize not only your own expertise but also the expertise of others. You bring together other experts in your industry and you simply interview them on particular topics or sub topics that fall under the overall topic or theme of your book.

You can do these interviews over the phone, over Skype or even in person. You'll record these interviews then get them transcribed and edited and each interview becomes a chapter.

Say for example you're writing a book on online marketing and you split the chapter into seven different chapters covering seven different sub topics within the realm of online marketing.

You could then get six other experts and each expert would cover one topic. Create a set of questions, record the interviews, get them transcribed and edited and hey presto you're done.

Simple as that.

Two BIG advantages to this method are:

1. You don't have to create all the content yourself
2. You get to tap into the network of your chosen experts and they may help you promote the book.

This method was actually something I used years ago to create one of my first information products. I interviewed 13 of the best fitness experts and created the Our Brains Your Fitness guide to fitness and health.

So how do you go about doing this?

Well once you have your core topic – make a list of 20-50 experts you would like to have in the book. I say 20-25 experts because when you start reaching out to your chosen experts, some won't respond, some will respond but don't want to contribute and others will. Generally you'll end up with the right amount in the end.

Google will be your best friend here. Simply search in Google for experts in your field. Alternatively you could use some services like HARO (Help A Reporter Out) where you can post your request and experts will seek you out.

The Interview Method is a great method to use because you get to leverage other people's content and expertise plus you get to expand your own network.

Also, if you're worried about whether or not you're an expert you can tap into the expertise of others and by the power of association you'll be putting yourself in the same brackets as those you have in your book. It's very, very powerful indeed.

The One Problem – One Solution Method

This one is pretty straightforward and very, very powerful too. This method is becoming very popular online, for online products, eBooks, online courses and things like that but it works equally well for business and lead generation books.

Think about your target audience and all the problems they have (as it relates to your product service). The one problem, one solution method simply takes these ideas and presents a solution to them. But the key is focusing on just one of their problems.

Your book will usually focus on their (your target markets) biggest problem or the one that's going to give them the biggest pay off if they solve it.

Like Zig Ziglar said *"you can get everything you want in life by help people get what they want."*

And solutions to problems are something what EVERYONE wants.

The more specific you are here the better. Instead of doing a book on online advertising (which obviously still has merit) if you were utilizing the one problem one solution method you might make the focus of your book Facebook Marketing for Dentists. See I'm choosing one problem a target market has (not being able to market online) and getting really specific in that area.

Another example is from a book on Direct Mail called *The Direct Mail Solution* by Craig Simpson. Now, Craig could of went out and published a book on marketing as a whole, but he's a direct mail guy and he's knows his target audience have a lot of problems with Direct Mail so he put together a comprehensive book and guide to using Direct Mail profitably (solving the problem).

It' a book I definitely recommend by the way.

Basically he went deep into one problem and he solved it for his target audience. You can do the exact same thing.

What are some of the problems that your target audience is having as it relates to your product or service?

Pick one of those problems dive deep into it, go into as much detail as possible on it and provide a solution to it.

Going back to the example I mentioned earlier of Facebook Advertising – this idea would fall under the One problem One Solution method.

One problem people have with Facebook advertising is they simply don't know how to use it or create ads and campaigns that are profitable.

My book would solve that one problem – I won't talk about Google Adwords, SEO, Direct Mail, or any other channels and I won't be talking about free methods on Facebook.

Just Facebook Advertising.

That's the beauty of the one problem, one solution method.

One tip here and actually a tip for all of your writing be it this method, the other methods, a blog post, an article, an email, letter or even a status update write for ONE PERSON. Write specifically for your most IDEAL client / customer.

The Personal Story With Lesson Method

This method is exactly as the title suggests. Your book's core theme will be that of a personal story with an over arching message. You're going to be sharing your personal story and the lessons you've learned from that story or personal journey.

What life experiences of have you gone through in your life? What have you achieved? What are some of the biggest challenges and obstacles you have overcome?

And what were the lessons you learned from them?

My first book *Your Elephant's Under Threat* combined a lot of these methods. The large proportion of my first book your Elephants Under Threat is very personal as it shares all of things I went through (good and bad).

Things like getting bullied growing up, my dad's health problems serving my inspiration, my volunteering in South America, my run ins with the law, problems with alcohol all the way to starting my business and everything that came with that.

The thing is out of all of my books published so far, my first book which is the most personal has received the highest praise from clients, customers and even those I look up to – like Dan Kennedy, Brian Tracy, Tom Hopkins, Nick Nanton and Clate Mask of Infusionsoft to name a few.

I'm nigh on certain part of this is because of the very personal nature of the book. When you openly share yourself with others (warts and all) you bond them to you in a way that traditional content cannot.

That bond is so strong because not only are you sharing your experience, you're sharing part of who you are and you're sharing the lessons you've learned in a way other people can learn from them, but you're getting very personal with them and you bond with them on a whole other level. It's not just about content anymore.

I've had people contact me saying they've gone through similar things, I've had clients and partnerships start because of my personal sharing in books that would NEVER have started otherwise.

It really is that powerful. It comes down to aged old, clichéd saying of *"People don't do business with a business, they do business with people."*

The personal story method might be the one you find the hardest, not because it's hard mechanically but you may need to get out of your own way before you're willing to openly share the good and bad of everything that is you.

Remember these questions: What challenges have you gone through? What obstacles have you overcome? What life experiences have you experienced that your target audience could learn from?

You can be as personal as you want to be, you can hold things back of course but the more personal you are, the more of a bond you'll create with your target audience.

The Gap in Market Method:

This method involves a strategy that you should use before you ever come up with a product/service idea but it works amazingly well for a book too.

Basically you look at what's out there in the marketplace, not just in books but in other arenas as it relates to your product or service.

There are three areas I recommend you look:

A. Amazon (or another global marketplace)
B. Forums specific to your market / industry
C. Your own customers.

The process you will follow is pretty similar for each.

We'll start with Amazon.

A. Amazon (or another global marketplace)

Heard of Amazon? Of course you have. Well much like Google – Amazon is a search engine but there's one key difference.

People search on Amazon to BUY things. Obviously people search to buy on Google also but Amazon is purpose built by the genius that is Jeff Bezos (who I recommend you study by the way).

The book *The Everything Store* by Brad Stone is one you should definitely add to your library. It paints a very clear picture on how of one of the most relentless entrepreneurs of our time, operates.

Due to Amazon being a buyers paradise, it contains a treasure throve of information, market research and customer insight that would cost you tens upon tens of thousands to obtain on your own.

Don't limit yourself to Amazon either; you can also use online course marketplaces like Udemy.com, Lynda.com, and Skillshare.com

Here are the steps you will follow:

1. Search for magazines, book titles and products related to your core idea or topic for your book.

First and foremost don't get dismayed by a lot of results, and don't consider this competition.

Lots of existing books, information, guides and more on a topic isn't a bad thing – it's a GREAT thing. It means there's a HUNGRY MARKET for your topic. This is key.

Remember, pioneers end up with arrows in their back.

2. In the search results you want to filter by the most popular results.

Here, you're going to look at the reviews from buyers.

Don't just look at the positive feedback either. Look at the most positive AND negative feedback. This is absolute gold I'm giving you here by the way.

3. Make note of all this positive and negative feedback.

The people who left positive feedback will be telling you everything they loved and the people who left negative feedback will be telling you what they didn't like and what they WISHED was in it.

4. Repeat the process for as many titles, books, courses as you need to.

You'll know when you have enough – and I've no doubt you'll find some absolute nuggets you would never have thought of on your own.

B. Forums specific to your market / industry

The process for forums is pretty similar to the Amazon method. Here you will dive deep into the most popular forums in your industry.

A forum is basically an online community where people who have the same interest (and problems) congregate. If you're not sure what forums to search in, the easiest thing you can do is go to Google and search: "your industry" forums.

For example search: retirement planning forums if you're a financial planner.

1. Make a list of the most popular forums.

You can see how popular the forums are by checking how many members and posts there are (usually listed at bottom of the forum) or you can check how much traffic the forum is getting by plugging it into Similarweb.com

2. Once you have your list start going through each forum, looking at the most popular posts and "threads" as they're known.

Sort the forum posts and threads by the highest number of replies to make sure you're focusing on the most popular.

3. Make a note of all the frequently asked questions and answers as well as any other information you think is pertinent to your book.

By the way, this process is something I recommend doing for all of the methods I'm walking you through because it gives you a direct line to your potential customers.

C. Your Own Customers

Finally, I recommend you talk to your own customers.

If you have a blog or a newsletter announce or tease the idea of your book and ask them for help.

You'd be surprised how many people will respond looking to help you. Ask them what their biggest challenge is as it relates to your product/service/book idea.

You could simply call or email your customers personally too. Interview your best customers – find out why they chose to do (and keep doing) business with you.

Offer them a free copy of the book if they'll provide a testimonial for it or a review for it.

Summary:

As you can see – there's nothing particularly complicated about any of this is there? Sure there's some work involved but you knew that already right?

I know for a fact you could take one of those methods and run with it and get amazing results. You'll have your book created in no time at all. The next step is when you've got your content created, is to start finalizing your book. That's what I'm going to talk about next.

My full Expert Authority Formula training, course and done for you resources go into much more detail and gives you the exact steps to follow as well as the fill in the blanks templates to make implementing a breeze. It all starts with the Expert Authority Thud Factor webinar. Be sure to register at:

www.expertauthorityformula.com/register

JOHN MULRY, MSC

PART IV: Finalizing Your Book

Once you have the core content of your book created now is the time to add the finishing touches. Don't worry too much if your manuscript is a bit of mess. That's what an editor is for ☺

In this section we're going to discuss a couple of key elements to finalizing your book.

1. Book Cover Design
2. Editing
3. ISBN
4. Design and Printing Preparation
5. Fulfillment
6. Done For You Services

Let's look at each of these in detail:

1. Book Cover Design

Your book cover design is very important as it's the first thing people will see when they look at your book. The truth is we do judge books by their cover and if you skimp here you'll pay dearly.

Your cover should be eye catching, it should intrigue the reader and want to make them pick it up and read it. The design should reach out to your audience. Your design file needs to be created so the end result looks and feels great. If the artwork is not good, it does not matter how good the printing is, it will not look good.

Some key tips:

I.   Don't be afraid to spend money on a great cover. Utilize places like Upwork.com, 99Designs.com, Freelancer.com or a local (and talented) graphic designer with book cover design experience.

II.   Make sure you cover is striking and it demands attention. Look at the books you've bought yourself – what do you like about the covers?

III. Sometimes, less is better. A simple cover can work wonders too. I made the cover for his second book *The Truth!* in Photoshop in about 10 minutes. But it's striking and really stands out a mile.

IV.   You want to think about the size of the book when creating the cover. Business books are portrait with popular sizes being 5.5 x 8.5, 6 x 9, 7 x 10, 8 ½ x 11. Another great approach that people have been using is a smaller size 5.25 x 8".

V.   Color choices – You will want to research the colors you pick for the cover as they can have a positive or negative impact on a consumers reaction to the book. A good designer will be able to help you create a concept using great printing techniques that will make your book stand out and be remembered.

VI.   Treatments for the cover – Your cover can be printed with many different techniques, it can be full color, it can be foil stamped (many different options from colors to holographic foils), and you can raise the print or press it in (embossing or debossing). Finally the coating on the book cover will determine the feeling a person has when they touch the book. Film laminations that come in gloss, matte, soft touch, gritty finishes will influence your buyer's reaction to the book.

VII. Create several cover concepts and show them to associates, friends and customers that will give you honest feedback.

2. Editing Your Book

Professional editors are essential to review your manuscript, check it for grammar, punctuation and spelling. If you need your book indexed, generally that requires a special editor.

It is never a good idea to try and edit your own book; you need someone who can be objective. This way the final manuscript will be perfect and ready to go to the designer to layout your pages.

Again think about using the online freelance websites like Upwork.com or Freelancer.com, you'll find lots of cost effective editors there and you could save yourself a tonne of money by going with a freelance editor versus a traditional one.

3. ISBN Number

Every book needs an ISBN number. The best and easiest place to get an ISBN number is at Nielsonisbnstore.com – You buy a single ISBN number or a block of 10.

4. Design and Printing Preparation

Once you have your book manuscript and cover created it need to be formatted properly for printing.

There's a couple of thing you need to be aware of.

Determine the size of your book i.e., 5.5 x 8.5, 6 x 9, 8 ½ x 11. You will need to have a front cover, back cover and a spine. If the design goes to the edge of the paper it needs to extend 1/8" past the trim edge, this is known as bleed.

Do not have your type going right to the edge; it could possibly be cut off.

It is best to give the printer or publisher a press ready PDF that is "CMYK", 300 dpi, with crops and bleed for the entire cover.

When it comes to page layout and design, there are 3 elements to be aware of.

The header, this is the information at the top of the page, the footer, this is the information at the bottom of the page and finally the text. The selection of serif or sans serif fonts, the size of the type, line spacing, and margins must all be taken into consideration when laying out the book.

It is a good idea to go to a book store or library and look through many books to see the styles you like and copy them in your book.

5. Fulfillment

I will be covering using Amazon for book fulfillment in a later section but for now we want to focus on using a traditional printer for fulfillment. If you are self publishing a book, start with a short run on the books.

Select a printer you can talk to and specializes in working with people who are self publishing.

Have the printer look at your files, give you paper samples and show you different types of covers they have done. Make sure they can print, laminate and bind in house. This ensures you will get the book when you want it and if there is a problem you can hold them accountable.

There are different types of printers for books. Find out what they specialize in. Things to consider are: size of book, hardcover vs. soft cover, color insides vs. black and white printing on demand vs. large quantities. These are all factors in selecting the best printer for your project.

WATCH OUT: You will be responsible for the marketing of your book regardless of what you are told. The printer's expertise is printing.

I will be covering the marketing of your book in the next section.

Make your life easy. Don't think you are saving money by having your books on a shelf at home and filling your own orders. It is a lot of work.

You will have to go to the post office (hopefully every day), but you will have to package your orders using the best envelopes or mailers, get the tracking information, figure out the best method to send it in the US or internationally.

Find a printer that specializes in information marketing they will be able to print and fulfill your orders. They'll be able to do it, cheaper than you can do it and more importantly you will be able to spend your time on the most profitable tasks in your business.

6. DONE-FOR-YOU services

We have been discussing the "Do-It-Yourself" approach. If it sounds like a lot of work and you don't want to be bothered you can find people or businesses that have a done for you approach.

They handle everything, finding a designer, editor, printing, fulfillment and distribution, getting your book on Amazon and into bookstores. Helping you create a website, building a prospect list, marketing funnel, landing pages, direct mail to your audience.

And if your cash rich and time poor you could go all the way and get a ghost writer to write your book for you.

If this is you and you like the idea of being an Expert Authority but you're short on time you can find out more about my DONE-FOR-YOU Expert Authority Formula program at the end of this book.

PART V: Promoting and Marketing Your Book to Get You Clients

Once your book is finished, edited, and complete with a striking, attention grabbing cover you should do two important things.

Make sure you don't skip either.

1. Give yourself a pat on the back

Seriously, while I believe everyone has at least one book in them, only a very small percentage of people ever get around to writing one.

Obviously the methods and strategies I've outlined for you in this book will make writing your book infinitely easier (you do agree don't you?). It doesn't take away from the fact when your book is finished you should be VERY PROUD of yourself.

2. Realise writing your book is only STEP 1!

I know, I know, it sucks. But it's the truth. You want me to be straight with you don't you? Writing your book is only the beginning. The real fun starts afterwards and in this section I'm going to explore some different methods for PROMOTING YOUR BOOK.

Much like in business – it's hardly ever a case of *"build it and they will come"*.

It's actually more like, build it specifically for a hungry market, find and attract them, entice them, wow them, convert them, keep them, champion them, maven them.

The good thing is that with a book you have a whole world of possibilities available to you.

We're going to start by quickly going over the differences, advantages and disadvantages to publishing your book the "new" way of the "traditional" way.

By "new" way I mean by self publishing and by "traditional" I mean through a traditional publisher.

Both have distinct advantages and disadvantages.

The advantages of going with a traditional publisher are:

- They will handle most of the marketing and promotion for you.
- They have massive distribution networks.
- You can get a LOT of exposure for your book fast.
- It's pretty much hands off for you.

The disadvantages to traditional publishing are.

- It's EXTREMELY hard to get your book noticed by publishers let alone published. They get 1000's of proposals every week.
- You lose the control of your book – the publisher can dictate what goes and what stays in your book.
- Your royalties are usually very low.
- You have to submit a long winded proposal with absolute no guarantee of being accepted.
- You have and show a strong marketing plan for your book and backup that you too can bring in LOTS of sales or they won't look at you.

- It's a long and tedious process.

I am not against the traditional method – not by a long shot. If you can secure a publishing deal I'd highly recommend you take it but because the process can be so long, tedious and more often than not a fruitless exercise, I recommend (at least at the beginning) self publishing your book.

The advantages of doing so are:

- It's quick and relatively easy process.
- You can use print on demand services like Amazon, LULU, NOOK and others.
- You can get started with this process for free or low cost.
- You have complete control over your book.
- You a higher royalty per book.
- You get your book published ASAP.

The disadvantages are:

- You're in charge of all of the marketing and promotion.
- You will be hands on in the process (unless you use a fulfillment center).

Again, because this will be a business book you're publishing with the goal of getting you clients, I wouldn't be turned off by the prospect of having to market your book yourself.

If you follow the steps laid out for you in previous sections, your book will be in big demand and as you'll discover, your book will open a lot of doors for you.
One of the best methods you can use for your book is by publishing it on Amazon.

But there are PERILS of using just Amazon and that's what I want to discuss next.

Tapping into the Buyer's Marketplace:

Once your book is finished, one of the first things you want to do is list it on Amazon.

You can do so a number of ways.

You can list the eBook version of your book on Kindle and you can list the physical copy of your book on Amazon (and other marketplaces) through CreateSpace, Amazon's print publishing arm.

Listing your book on Amazon is great for a number of reasons:

1. You get your book in front of a much wider audience.
2. People trust Amazon – and have no problem spending money there.
3. You have the opportunity to list your book on Kindle through the KDP (Kindle Direct Publishing) and do special promotions to drive downloads and sales for your book.
4. Amazon handles all the printing and fulfillment – and you get a royalty. The royalty percentage depends on the pricing of your book and where the

book is sold. All of this is explained clearly when you set your book up on Amazon.

Amazon is a fantastic marketplace but there is ONE big drawback:

The big problem with Amazon is when someone buys your book, you don't know who they are, or where they are. Amazon gets the buyer – not you.

Obviously it's great you sold your book on Amazon, possibly to someone who wouldn't of bought otherwise but unless you give your readers every opportunity to take the next step (say for example visiting your website to get bonus content), like I have in this book) you never get to engage with that buyer or add more value to them.

One thing I'd like to stress is you don't want to bombard them with too many call to actions in the book.

I hope you'd agree that in this book while I have mentioned my advanced Expert Authority Formula program and our other resources frequently – I have only done so when it makes sense to do so.

The reason I do this is threefold and the mere fact I'm revealing all of this "inside baseball" should show how serious we are about helping you.

1. I want to add more value to you.
2. I want to take you from a book reader and turn you into a lead I can follow up with.
3. I want to offer you more useful resources, guidance and services.

I'm up front about all three because it's important you understand the strategy behind writing your book.

While some people will automatically self select and ascend on to further training, products and done for you services, you can't assume just because someone reads your book they will automatically want to buy more and more.

Sometimes we need gentle cues and reminders about what to do next. Other times we need to be held by the hand and led to the next steps. You are no different and either will be your readers.

So while one of Amazon's big drawbacks is that you don't get the buyer, you can give your Amazon readers every opportunity to take the next step in your sales process.

You can do this a number of ways:

A. Offer them exclusive bonus – sending them to an "optin page" (a page where they can give you're their contact details in exchange for access to the book bonuses) on your site exclusively for readers.
B. Offer them bonus training or advanced training.
C. Make it clear in your "Next Steps" chapter what they should do next.
D. Ask them to submit questions they might have by email and give them your email address.

There's no hard and fast rule here, just make sure you offering value at every stage of your sales process – as long as you're helping your readers and prospects at each stage – that's all that matters.

And don't be afraid to make the offer either. Like this one.

So far if you're enjoying this book –we highly recommend you get access to our bonus training and our advanced Expert Authority Formula program. You can access them at www.expertauthorityformula.com/register

Nice and simple call to action right?

As well as Amazon – don't neglect the other marketplaces like LULU and NOOK. While they may not be as popular as Amazon, they still have a lot of buyers over there and you should consider listing your book on their marketplaces too.

The BIG mistake a lot of authors and publishers make...

All of these marketplaces like Amazon, LULU and NOOK are fantastic but if you solely focus on listing your book there you're missing out big time.

Remember the goal of your book is to get you clients' right?

One way you can ensure that you give yourself every chance of turning your buyers into clients is by building your own book marketing asset, system or funnel.

This is what I'm going to walk you through now.

Having fun so far?

Building an automated book marketing funnel that generates leads on near autopilot...

One of the best things you can do for your book is to build a marketing funnel for it.

A book marketing funnel is essentially an online system you build (or have someone build for you) that automates the process of you:

1. Generating leads for your book
2. Converting those leads into book buyers
3. Ascends those book buyers into repeat buyers or clients.

This isn't just a website however. While it does contain web pages, they are specific types of pages strategically designed and stringed together in order to sell your books and generate you clients.

I'll be walking you through examples of my own book funnels in a minute but some of the main advantages of building your very own book funnel are;

1. You get to engineer your book marketing system so it leads to you achieving your goal of getting clients.

2. You know who your buyers are and you can follow up with them.
3. You can make more offers to your buyers and thus increase your average transaction size of your book buyers.
4. You can add passive income to your business.
5. You'll be building your database of buyers.

If you're thinking that you've never created a book marketing funnel before or you think that's its way too technical for you – you could always hire someone to do it for you.

I have a DONE-FOR-YOU book marketing funnel service and details of that are at the end of this book. I'm not cheap, but as the saying goes – you get what you pay for.

It is something you can do yourself of course, there are a number of tools and software available you can use.

Like anything there'll always be an investment – of time or money. If money is tight you can always build it yourself but this will take time (and possibly learning). If money is not a problem, time might be and in this case you would be better served getting someone to do it for you.

What will your book marketing funnel look like and consist of?

Here you have a number of options and you while you can be creative it's best to follow what works.

Here are some example layouts for your book funnel:

1. Free Chapter Offer > Full Book Offer > Advanced Training > Free Consult > New Client
2. Free Book (eBook Version) > Physical Copy > Free Consult > New Client
3. Free Physical Copy > Book sent with Shock N Awe Packet > New Client
4. Free Physical Copy (Just Pay Shipping) > Advanced Training > Continuity Program > New Client

These are just some examples – you can mix and match. Test out different offers and strategies until you find which one works for you.

Let's look at some actual examples of some book funnels we have created.

These are some of my own as well as some client funnels I have created:

On the following pages you'll see some examples of real life book funnels that have been proven to convert website visitors to leads, leads to buyers and buyers to clients.

The funnels are the following:

1. **The Truth! – John Mulry**
2. **Your Elephant's Under Threat – John Mulry**
3. **Consumer's Guide to Investment Real Estate – Jim Toner**
4. **Five Deadly Sins - Steven Lazarus**

I wanted to show you real life examples so you can see what the actual funnels look like.

Model these because they work!

The Truth! Book Funnel

Fig. 1: The Truth! Homepage

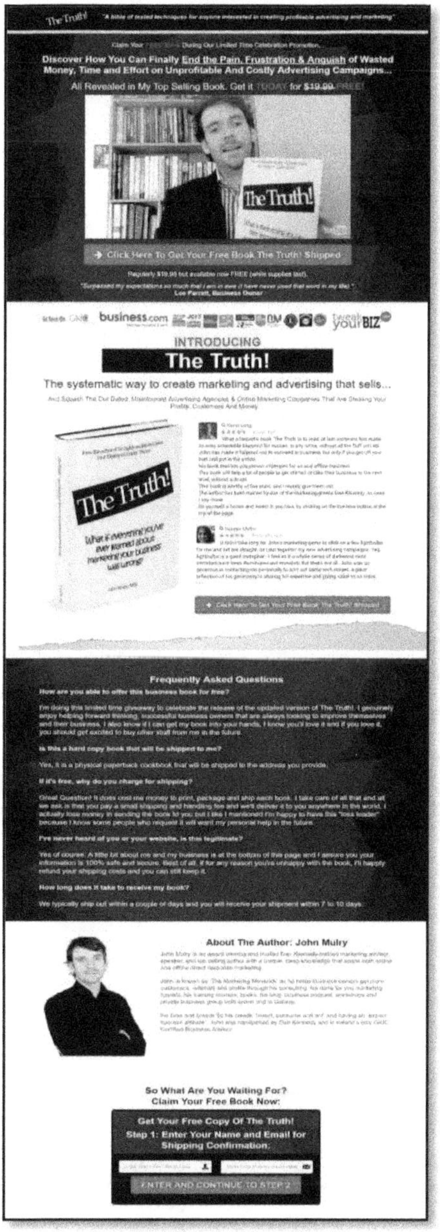

Fig. 2: The Truth! Order Form Page

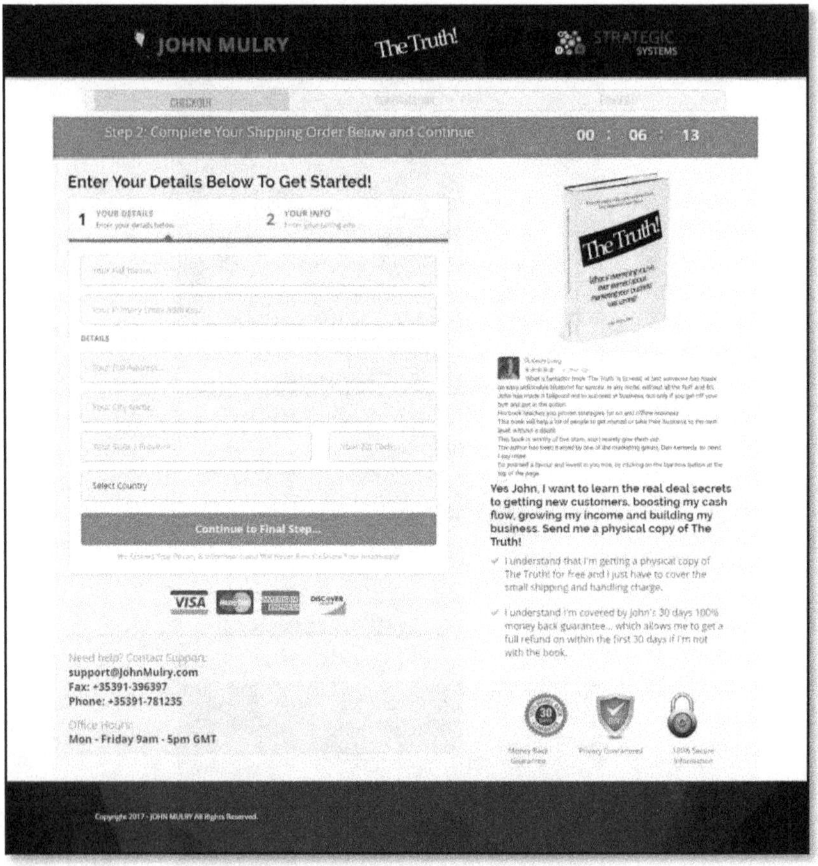

Fig 3: The Truth! Upsell Page

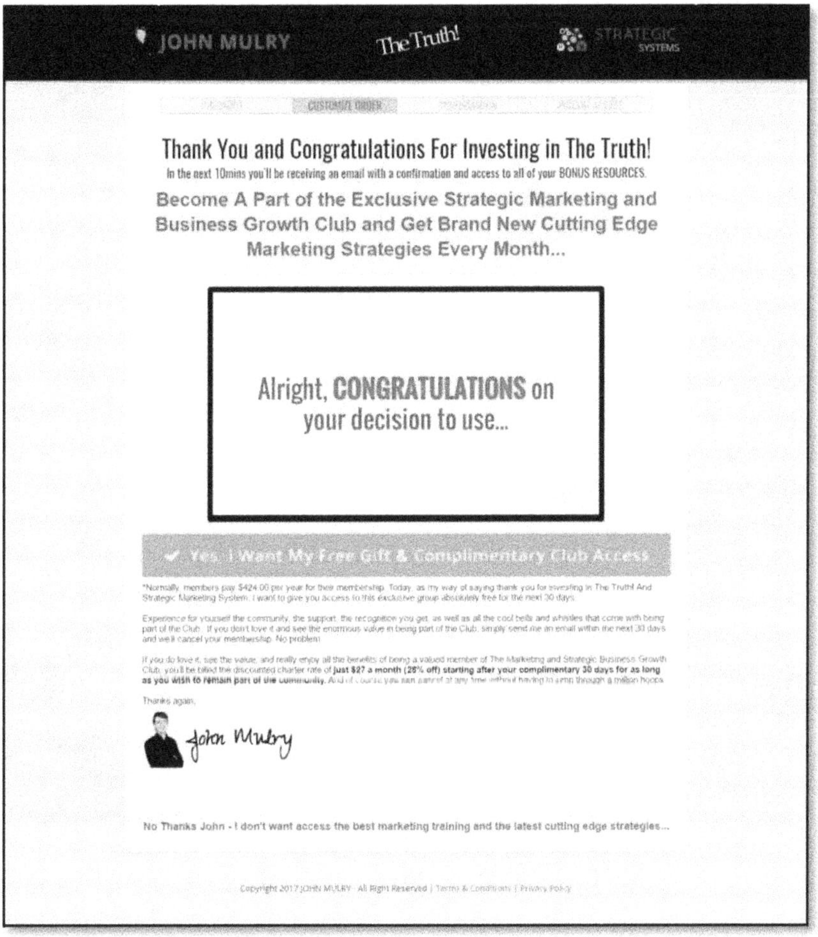

Fig 4: The Truth! Thank You Page

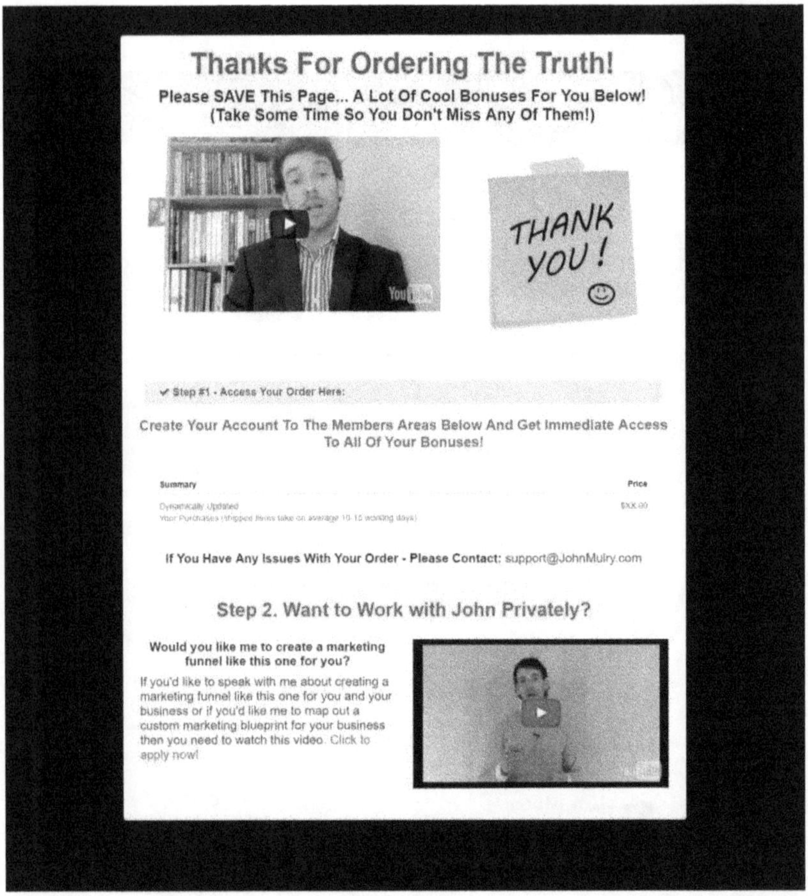

Your Elephant's Under Threat Funnel

Fig 5: Your Elephant's Under Threat Homepage

Fig 6: *Your Elephant's Under Threat Upsell Page*

Fig 7: *Your Elephant's Under Threat Upsell 2 Page*

Fig 8: Your Elephant's Under Threat Thank You Page

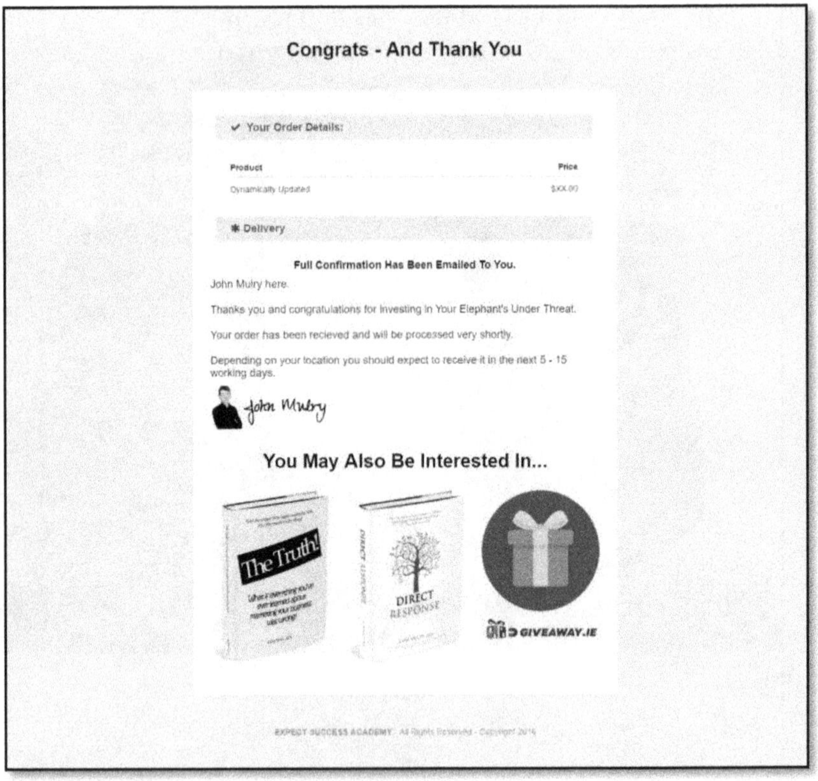

Consumer's Guide to Investment Real Estate Funnel

Fig 9: Consumer's Guide to Investment Real Estate Homepage

Fig 10: Consumer's Guide to I.R.E. Physical Copy Offer Page

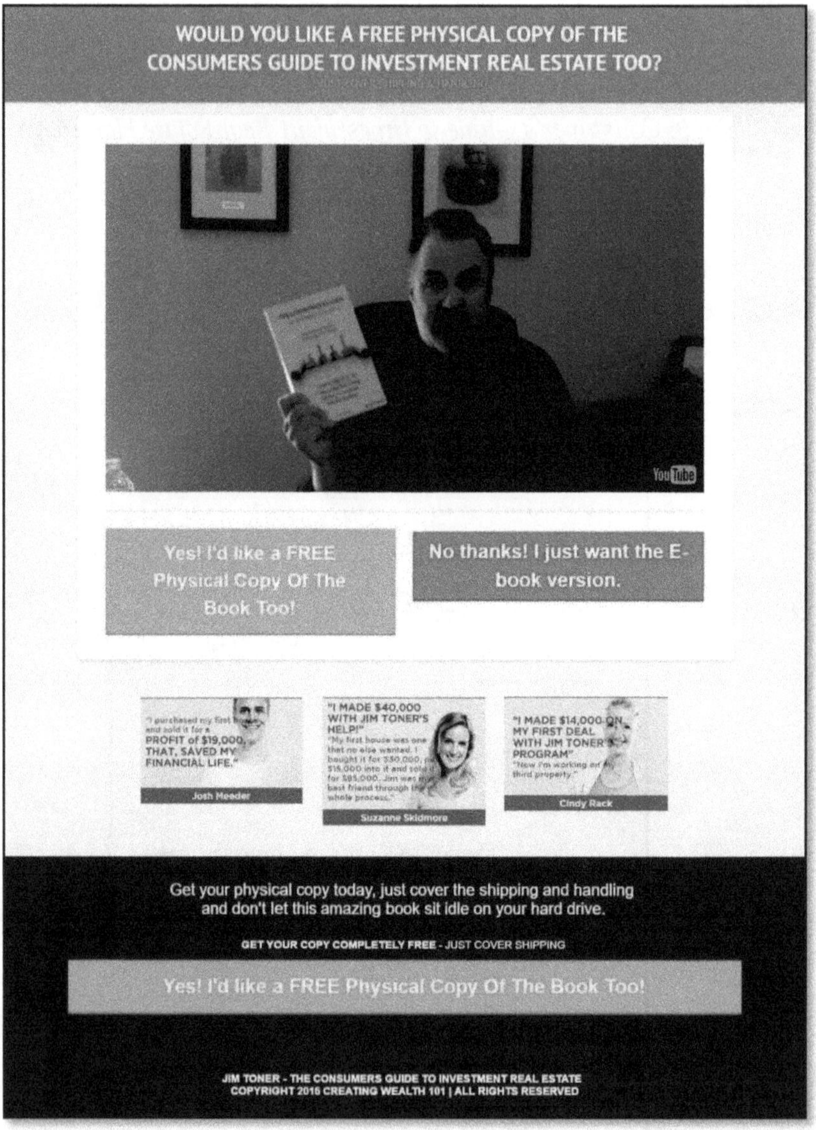

Fig 11: Consumer's Guide to I.R.E. Order Page

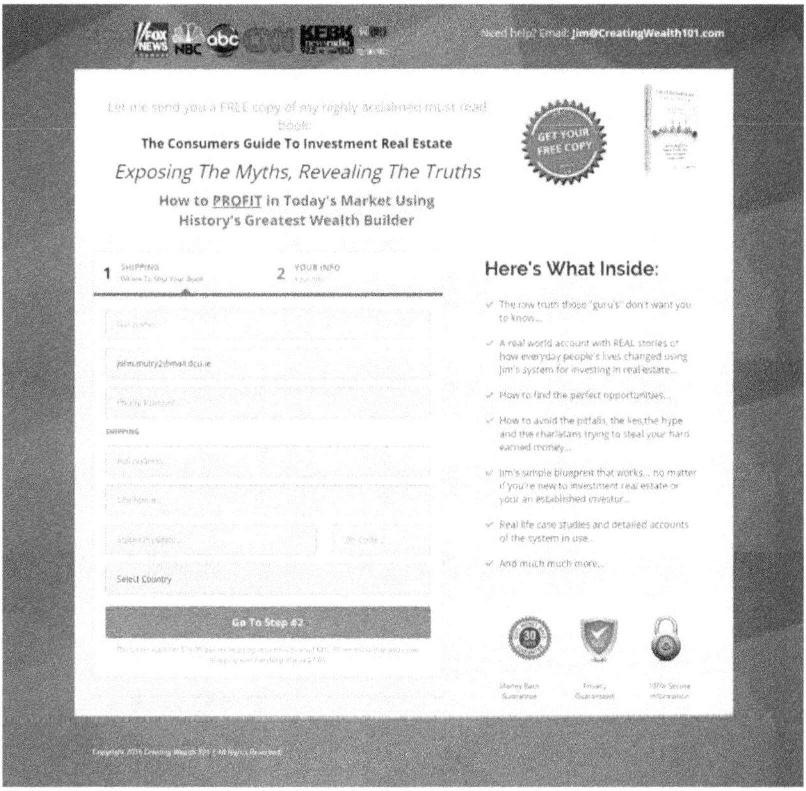

Fig 12: Consumer's Guide to I.R.E. Thank You Page

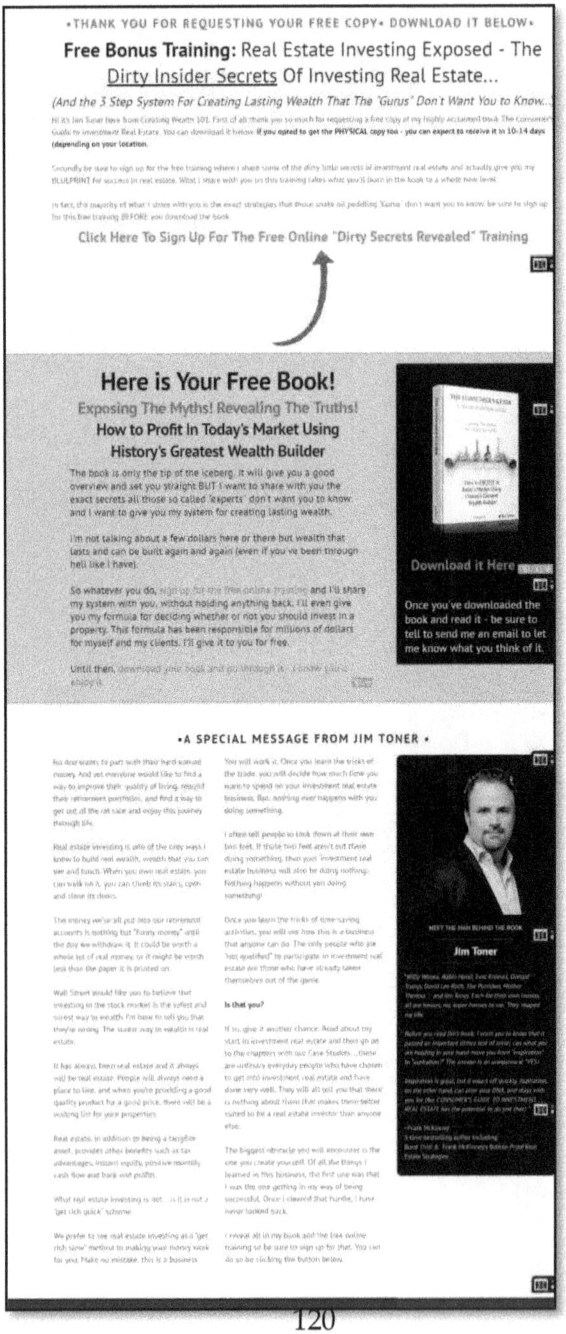

Five Deadly Sins Funnel

Fig 13: Five Deadly Sins Homepage

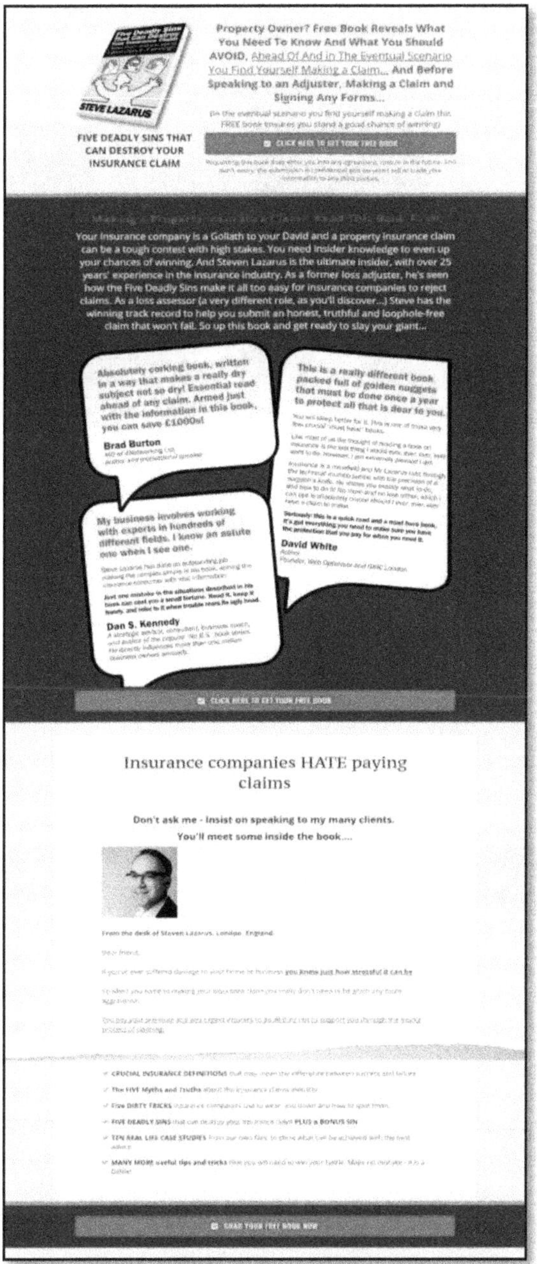

Fig 14: Five Deadly Sins Physical Offer Page

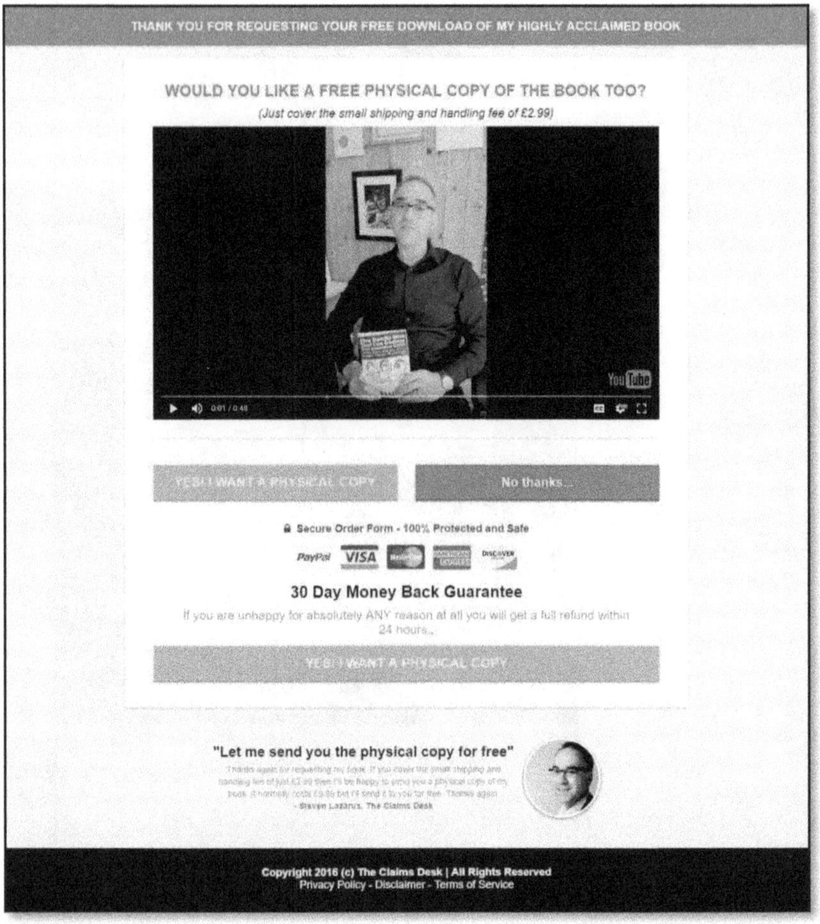

Fig 15: Five Deadly Sins Order Page

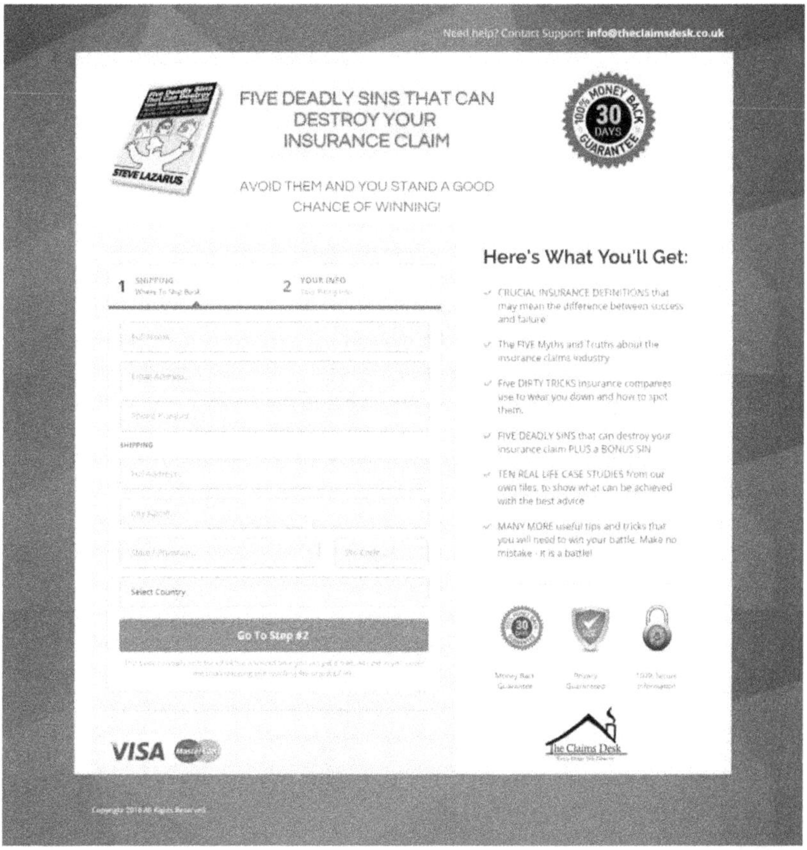

Fig 16: Five Deadly Sins Thank You + Next Steps

Thanks! You Can Download Below!

You've made an excellent decision that could save you £000s!

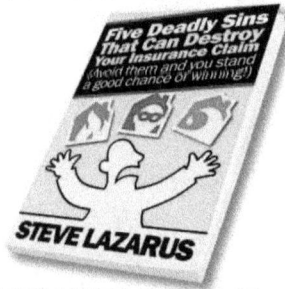

Click Here to Download Your Book

If you opted to get the physical copy of the book it will be mailed to you within the next 5 working days by first class mail. When you get it, open it immediately and absorb every word. It could save you £1,000's...

If your insurance claim is urgent - don't wait - reach out to immediately by calling 020 8906 0098 or 07782 19 54 55 or emailing me on info@theclaimsdesk.co.uk

Thanks again,
Steven Lazarus

The Claims Desk

Now you've seen examples of what some book funnels look like, I'm hoping you're starting to see the bigger picture of what your book (and the marketing of your book) can mean for you and your business.

But I'm not done yet – I want to share a couple of other examples and strategies you can use, to get exposure and clients with your book.

I'm going to start with a twist on the DREAM 100 strategy.

Your DREAM 100 Book Strategy

This "DREAM 100" strategy is an adapted strategy I learned from Chet Holmes and the book *The Ultimate Sales Machine* – a must read book for every business owner.

Here's I've adapted Chet's strategy of reaching out to your dream 100 to instead reaching out to your DREAM 100 Distribution networks.

What I mean by distribution network is: anyone be they a peer, an influencer in your market or industry, or entity, publication, media outlet, magazine/newspaper outlet or any source that has the potential to open up the promotional floodgates for you and your book.

Here are the steps you could (and should take):

1. Make a list of up to 100 dream distribution networks for your business and your book.

Think in terms of relevant people, groups, outlets or organizations that you are affiliated with, would like to be affiliated with and that are somewhat related to you book, your book's topic or your business.

2. Send them your book

Send them a physical copy of your book in the post – yes you will have to spend money here but it will be oh so worth it.

3. Include a personal written letter specific to them.

You can use a rough draft on the following page as a template but be sure to customize it for each person / network. Make sure your letter is straight to the point but also personal and down to earth.

4. Ask them for help in the letter

You're not going to push them or be salesy in your letter. You're going to ask them for help. Why? Well you do want help for one and two – people love helping other people.

Not everyone will respond to you but that's ok.

5. Follow up with them.

You're not going to just send one letter, one shot, hit and hope Hail Mary style marketing is a waste of time and money.

You're going to follow up with them. And follow up multiple times. I recommend anywhere from 3 to 12 times. You could do three standard letters and then send them a monthly quirky newsletter on your progress.

Include articles and information that'll help them – make it interesting, build a relationship with them with no expectation of return and you will flourish.

I highly recommend you use the DREAM 100 strategy you will make more contacts, widen your network and expand your books horizon wider than you could ever do on your own.

On the following page is a sample letter you can use a template:

****

Hi _____

I know you're super busy so I'm going to keep this short. I'm a massive fan of you/your podcast/your magazine/newsletter/books etc.

My favourite piece of yours is that article / book / video / interview you did on _____. It really helped me to _____

As you can see I've enclosed a copy of my book
_____

You don't know this but you've played a massive part in helping me write this.

The books main focus is to help people who are struggling with _____ and want to _____.

You're someone whose opinion I really value and I'd love if you could point me in the right direction of what you would do if you were in my position with this book?

Is there anything you would do if you were me?

You can reach me by phone on 123456789 or by email on youremail@email.com

Thanks for reading,
Your Name

P.S. I think you'll love what's on page XY – I know you'll definitely relate to it ☺

****

Now obviously, that letter needs some tweaking but it's a great starting point.

Please only reach out to people or organizations using this template with who you've genuinely have an interest in, are or could be affiliated with or have learned from.

By all means reach out to other as well but change the letter slightly.

Next up I'll be discussing a simple but powerful method you can use to systematically start attracting clients with your book.

"Planting The Farm" With Your Book

Planting the farm is a term I first heard from my mentor Dan Kennedy. It refers to creating a multi step multimedia system for reaching out to cold prospects, getting them to raise their hand and tell you they're interested in doing business with you.

Typically you would have a three step direct mail system – with three letters – each linked and each subsequent letter would refer to the previous.

The goal of this campaign is to generate leads for your business, offer them something of value. You get them to raise their hand telling you they're interested then you would follow up with them and ascend them to one of your products / services.

You may be thinking: *"Who the hell do I target?"*

You would target your customer lists with this campaign or you could go to a list broker and rent a list (or use lists.nextmark.com) to find the perfect list for your business.

Not a lot of people know about lists.nextmark.com – they're the search engine of direct mail lists. No matter what your industry – you can find lists on there to suit your needs.

Whether you use your own list, a list broker, an endorsed mailing (where someone will mail out for you to their list) using a plant the farm sequence for your book is a great idea.

A "plant the farm" book offer, direct mail sequence is an excellent system to implement in your business for a number of reasons:

1. You get to tap into the power of direct mail – everyone is online and there's hardly any competition offline with direct mail.
2. You can access targeted lists quickly and inexpensively.
3. With the right offer/product/service afterwards your ROI can be off the charts.

Let's look at some numbers:

Assumptions:

1. Cost of direct mail piece is $1
2. Cost of list is $500
3. Cost to send book is $7
4. Your core offer is $5,000

Send this sequence to 1,000 prospects (three letters each) = $3,000.

Let's say each letter gets a meager 1% response.

That's 30 requests for your free book so that's 30 X $7 = $210 to send out the books.

If you just closed 10% of those into your high ticket program at $5,000 that's 3 new clients at $5,000 = $15,000

Total Cost: $3,710
Total Revenue: $15,000

Customers Acquired: 30

ROI = 404% For every $1 spent you generate $4.04

Can you see how powerful this "planting the farm" sequence is?

What if you got a 2% response?

What if you closed 50% of the people who responded.

This gets very sexy very fast ☺

Now if you're saying "I don't have a high ticket" program for $5,000 then you can plug in your own program costs or better yet CREATE A HIGH TICKET PROGRAM.

Your Book is Just The Entry Point

There's something I want to make clear is that your book is just the entry point.

The strategies I've been recommending have all involved using your book as the lead inn tool to help you get clients but the reality is, while your book WILL you get clients – that's not the only thing it can do for you.

It will inevitably lead to speaking engagements, both paid and free (both have merits) and this too will open a whole ream of opportunities for you (if you want them).

You'll be asked to talk about your book, you can take some of the core topics in your book and turn them into a presentation that you give where you sell your books at the end or you could sell your consulting / coaching at the end. The possibilities are endless.

You'll be invited on radio, interviewed by the press all of which can be leveraged as part of your marketing strategy in your business. Just remember – your book is just step 1.

In the next section I'll be talking about the secret sauce to your book.

This is the stuff that no one else dares share with you...

Guess that's why they call me *The Marketing Maverick*...

JOHN MULRY, MSC

PART VI: The Secret Sauce EXTRA Elements To Your Book...

In this section I'm going to walk you through some other elements to your book that will add a little bit of secret sauce to your book and the marketing of your book.

Once again these are all strategies that I have personally used and can verify work like crazy!

1. Make Money by Giving Your Book Away

Remember the goal of your book is to get clients right?

Well since this is the goal – you should NOT be worried about generating revenue from book sales.

You don't write your book to make money from book sales – you write your book to attract the right type of clients and that's how you make money (and a lot more than you'd make form just selling books).

That's why in the book funnel examples we laid out for you – we give our books away free or we just charge the shipping cost for the books.

The reason why we do this is generate the lead if we give it away free of generate a BUYER if we charge shipping.

The more interested people you can have in your database the more money you'll make. Obviously you'll have to follow up with your leads (through email and direct mail etc) but as long as you do so by building trust with them and adding value to them at every step, every time you make an offer to your database (and the offer makes sense) you will make sales.

2. Getting High Profile Endorsements

Another really nice touch to your book is some getting some high profile endorsements for your book.

Doing so is easier than you think.

Much like the DREAM 100 strategy – reach out to those who you have learned from, admire and look up to.

Be honest with them.

Go with the angle of how you can help them and always remember the acronym "WIIFM" which stands for: *"What's in it for me?"*

Plus, the worst thing they can say is no right? Or they mightn't say anything at all.

On the next page is a sample of an email I used to get an endorsement for my first book from Clate Mask – the co founder of Infusionsoft, one of the best marketing automation tools out there today.

Fig 21: Endorsement Request Sample

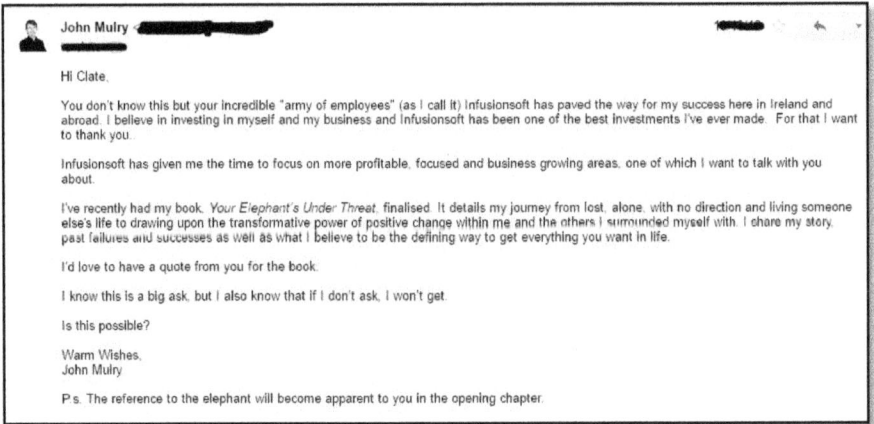

Hi Clate,

You don't know this but your incredible "army of employees" (as I call it) Infusionsoft has paved the way for my success here in Ireland and abroad. I believe in investing in myself and my business and Infusionsoft has been one of the best investments I've ever made. For that I want to thank you.

Infusionsoft has given me the time to focus on more profitable, focused and business growing areas, one of which I want to talk with you about.

I've recently had my book, *Your Elephant's Under Threat*, finalised. It details my journey from lost, alone, with no direction and living someone else's life to drawing upon the transformative power of positive change within me and the others I surrounded myself with. I share my story, past failures and successes as well as what I believe to be the defining way to get everything you want in life.

I'd love to have a quote from you for the book.

I know this is a big ask, but I also know that if I don't ask, I won't get.

Is this possible?

Warm Wishes,
John Mulry

P.s. The reference to the elephant will become apparent to you in the opening chapter.

3. Launch Your Book Locally and Leverage it Forever More

A really powerful strategy you can use with your book is to launch your book in a local bookstore where you live and leverage it like crazy.

Here's what you should do:

1. *Contact your local book store and tell them about your launch.*
2. *Send press releases to your local newspapers and radio.*
3. *Invite some high profile local celebrities to speak on your behalf.*
4. *Invite friends, family and clients to the launch night.*
5. *Hire a photographer and videographer to record the launch.*
6. *Enjoy the whole experience.*
7. *Share photos online and share the completed video everywhere (put it on your sales page for your book).*

Leverage the photos, the video, testimonials again and again online and offline in your marketing and advertising.

138

The Business Card With a Bang!

Another strategy you can use with your book is to turn up to every meeting with books instead of business cards.

Your book will become your business card and nothing says *"holy sh*t this guy is somebody I should listen to"* than handing out your very own book when they ask for your business card.

One thing is for certain, they won't throw your book away.

Most business cards are dumped or lost within a day of receiving, but a book has true value and will be kept or passed on to someone else.

Turn Your Book Into Passive Income

Like I keep stressing your book is just step 1.

There's so much potential available to you when you have your book finished. Heck it's why I have written so many and I'm only scratching the surface of my own potential and the potential of my books.

Once you've finished your book and you're actively promoting it and getting clients from it the logical next step is to turn your book into passive income.

How?

By turning your book into an online course that you can sell online.

Do the work once and profit from it again and again.

How do you do this?

Take your book chapters or sections and split them into modules – create a course with modules that expand on what you talk about.

Go deeper into each area and provide more resources be they videos, done for you templates, downloads and extras that make digesting and absorbing the information easier and faster.

The great thing about turning your online course is you set the price point.

The best online courses can range from anywhere from $49 to $1997.

And you can add this course to your online book funnel as an up sell and a certain percentage of people who buy your book will opt to invest in your course also thus increasing your average transaction size per customer.

I'm working on some advanced training on this especially for you so keep an eye out for a future update.

PART VII: Fast Track Your Results

I hope by now that you're absolutely chomping at the bit to start writing your own business book?

You are?

Great – I'm delighted.

If by some strange reason you're not – be sure to let me know.

Reach out to me at www.johnmulry.com and tell me why you're not – because you should be.

In this short book I laid out:

- Why you should write a business book
- How to write a business book, fast
- What you should write about
- How you can promote and leverage your book
- And much, much more.

If after all that you're not excited, I'm not sure what else I can do to convince you. Well there is one thing I can do...

I can fast track your results. How? By helping you...

I have put together a number of programs, packages and initiatives that are bespoke and tailored around your needs and your requirements.

Everyone is different and everyone has different needs/requirements etc.

Doing EVERYTHING on your own is hard and foolish.

I'm THE EXPERT at what I do so let me help you.

Essentially there are three ways I can help you:

1. **Expert Authority Formula Advanced Training & System**

Expert Authority Formula is my suite of advanced tools, training, templates and done for you resources to help you go from thinking of writing to actually writing in no time at all.

You can find out about my Expert Authority Formula Advanced Training System by registering for the THUD FACTOR method webinar at:

www.expertauthorityformula.com/register

2. **Expert Authority Formula 90 Day Coaching Program**

If you want me to 'hold your hand' and walk you through the process of implementation so you can:

- Get your book done as quickly as possible.
- Use it to get clients as quickly as possible (and get them BEFORE you even write a single word)

Then the Expert Authority 90 Day Coaching program is for you. Not only will you get full access to the Expert Authority Formula training and program but you'll have personal access to me to help you along every step of the way. By application only.

3. **Expert Authority Formula Completely A to Z Done For You Program**

If you want me to PERSONALLY help you with any or all of the elements of getting your book done, your funnel created and your marketing and advertising into high gear then our DONE-FOR-YOU packages are for you. This is perfect for those who are cash rich and time poor as I handle everything and essentially deliver your book, your funnel and campaigns and new clients on a silver plate. By application only.

One thing I'd like to stress if you're interested is I don't work with people who don't care about value and are only interested in getting the lowest price.

I am not the cheapest – but you get what you pay for.

Like my dad always used to say:

Cheap quality isn't great and great quality isn't cheap.

If you interested in finding out more about the Expert Authority 90 day coaching program or A to Z Done For You Program you can visit:

www.expertauthorityformula.com/apply

PART VIII: Your Next Steps...

I want to thank you for one getting this book and two for ACTUALLY taking the time to read it.

Investing time and money into your own learning is one of the best investments you can make.

INVEST is the 1st rule of success to me.

By getting this book in the first place you invested in yourself and if you're reading this I can hopefully assume that you not only invested in it, you also CONSUMED the information within these pages.

The second rule of success for me is CONSUME.

One must INVEST in themselves and then they must CONSUME.

Finally the last rule of success for me is to ACT.

I want you to ACT on what you've discovered inside these pages. And that doesn't necessarily mean enrolling in the Expert Authority Formula program or applying for my 90 Day Program or Done-For-You services.

Sure I'd love for you to apply but at the end of the day, whether it's with me or on your own I want you to ACT.

Take action.

INVEST, CONSUME and ACT and you're well on your way to achieving whatever it is you want to achieve.

Remember:

You don't necessarily get what you want and you don't necessarily get what you need, instead you get what you honestly and truly believe you deserve. In other words, you get what you expect, so why not EXPECT SUCCESS?

JM

About John Mulry

"Helping entrepreneurs become and be recognized as the EXPERT AUTHORITY in their marketplace...growing their business, client base and profits in the process."

John Mulry is an award winning and trusted marketing advisor, speaker, and Amazon #1 bestselling author with a unique, deep knowledge that spans both online and offline direct response marketing.

He helps coaches, consultants, trainers and professional service providers become the EXPERT AUTHORITY in their marketplace, and helps you get more customers, referrals and profits through his consulting, his done for you marketing funnels, his training courses, and programs.

When John first started his business rather than accept the status quo of the impending doom of the recession he sought out and has studied under some of the most world-renowned experts in business, direct response marketing and coaching. Experts including marketing legends Jay Abraham and Dan Kennedy, GKIC, business and personal development experts Tony Robbins, Dax Moy, and Emmy award winning movie director/branding agent Nick Nanton.

He lives and breeds by his creeds "invest, consume and act" and having an "expect success attitude". John was handpicked by Dan Kennedy and is Ireland's only GKIC Certified Business Advisor.

John has been featured as a guest contributor on numerous publications including Business.com, TweakYourBiz, NUI various newspaper and publications as well as been a guest speaker for the SCCUL Enterprise Centre, OMiG, JCI Galway, Galway Chamber of Ireland, the Elite Performance Academy, All-Ireland Summit, Plato and the Ennis Business Network.

In February 2013, John launched first book Your Elephant's Under Threat which received worldwide acclaim from some of the top business and marketing experts worldwide including: top selling author Brian Tracy, world renowned sales trainer Tom Hopkins, Infusionsoft founder Clate Mask, celebrity branding expert Nick Nanton as well as his own mentor and founder of GKIC, Dan Kennedy.

In May 2014 John won the JCI TOYP (Top Outstanding Young Persons Award) and has been a finalist in the JCI Young Entrepreneur of the year, OMiG marketer of the year and blogging awards.

In April 2015, John launched his second book The Truth! – which hit the top sellers three days in a row and received acclaim from customers and clients the world over. He has also launched numerous training programs, courses both online and offline.

In September 2016, John launched his 3rd book *Direct Response* and in October of 2016 he launched *The 7 Deadly Sins That Are Crippling Your Business.*

In October 20117 he launched his sixth book *Expert Authority* and his flagship Expert Authority Formula advanced training and 90 Day Coaching program.

For more information on John visit www.JohnMulry.com

For more information on the Expert Authority Formula visit www.expertauthorityformula.com/register

EXPERT AUTHORITY